Bending with the Breeze

STEVE RITCHIE

Typeset and designed by Raspberry Creative Type, Edinburgh

Be like a flower – strong enough to turn your face to the sun but flexible enough to bend with the breeze

This book is dedicated to my wife, Jane, whose support, wisdom and encouragement has helped me to remember to bend and flow and whose constant light has enabled me to never to lose sight of my path.

Preface

To get the most from this book, read it slowly, deliberately, with purpose.

Pause after each chapter, for a day, a week, a month; however long it takes to allow the messages of that chapter to sink in and become integrated into your life.

Only then should you move on to the next chapter.

Once you have completed the entire book, use the 30-Day Bending with the Breeze Challenge to put everything you have learned into practice.

Contents

INTRODUCTION

Why We Struggle,
Why We Push,
and Why We Break

Exploring our obsession
with persistence, and why
unbending willpower can
lead to burnout

Many of us drift through life without deliberately shaping our path, moving from one phase to another, reacting rather than leading. Others take a different approach. They set ambitious goals, craft detailed plans, and pursue success with laser-sharp focus. Yet for both groups, encountering an obstacle can feel the same.

What happens when your carefully crafted path falls apart? When limited resources, poor planning, or a lack of support transform what seemed like a clear road into a dead end?

What happens when you float around the next bend to realise you have run out of easy options and face a brick wall?

From childhood, we are taught that persistence holds the answer. We are told that *"If at first you don't succeed, try, try again"*. So, we try. We push. We force our way forward, convinced that sheer determination will unlock any door and break down any barriers.

But sometimes, the door won't budge. Sometimes, the barriers refuse to lift. Sometimes, despite our best efforts, we end up exhausted, frustrated, and completely stuck. **This is where traditional resilience thinking abandons us.**

We have learned to equate strength with standing firm, refusing to give in, refusing to bend, but if you've ever walked through a forest after a storm, you will have discovered a different truth.

The trees that fight the wind are the ones that break. The survivors are those that bend.

This book offers a different path to success: **Bending with the Breeze.**

Just as roots change direction when they hit solid rock and plants twist towards sunlight despite obstacles, we too can learn to move with life, not against it. Bending with the Breeze will teach you how to adapt when necessary, reroute intelligently, and stay committed to your purpose while remaining flexible in your actions.

This isn't about abandoning your goals. It's about refining your approach. It's about learning to sidestep the blow instead of absorbing its full force. It's about choosing strategic stillness over mindless persistence, and developing the ability to flex under pressure rather than breaking under it.

Bending with the Breeze is more than just a process - it's **a mindset.**

It is a way of thinking, acting, and moving through life with greater ease, deeper awareness, and more sustainable success.

So, as you embark on this journey, remember:

Be like a flower
— strong enough to turn your face to the sun,
but flexible enough to bend with the breeze.

1

Drifting Without Direction

Why aimlessness feels safe,
but ultimately steals our
momentum

*"If you don't know where you're going, any
road will get you there."*
LEWIS CARROLL

The Quiet Trap of Drifting

There's a certain ease in aimlessness.

No pressing obligations. No rigid expectations. No fear of failure.

Drifting can seem like freedom, at least on the surface. It lets us exist without dealing with difficult questions, making uncomfortable choices, or facing the possibility of mistakes.

However, beneath that ease lies something far more limiting. Stagnation.

Drifting doesn't lead us anywhere specific. It keeps us moving, but without momentum or purpose. While it gives the illusion of progress, there is little real advancement, and over time, this lack of direction drains us more than the fear of making a wrong decision ever could.

The Psychology of Drifting

Drifting often stems from something deeper than simple indecision. It's rooted in fear, uncertainty, and sometimes exhaustion.

1. The Fear of Failure

When we drift, we avoid the risk of failure. If we never commit to a decision, we never have to risk making a mistake. Ironically, however, aimlessness can become failure by default, simply because nothing happens.

2. The Paralysis of Too Many Choices

We live in an era of endless choices. Careers, lifestyles, creative activities - even how we prefer to take our coffee or which TV channel to watch - are all readily accessible to us. Instead of empowering us, this abundance often creates confusion and indecision, making us hesitant to choose anything at all out of fear of making the wrong choice.

3. The Comfort of Avoidance

Action requires effort. Commitment requires responsibility. So, we procrastinate and delay. We cling to familiar routines, convincing ourselves that we'll make a decision "soon," when really, we are just postponing discomfort indefinitely.

4. The Myth of Sudden Clarity

We tell ourselves that one day, clarity will come. The right path will appear. We'll wake up and suddenly know *exactly* what to do. But clarity isn't something we wait for - it's something we create through movement and engagement.

The Emotional Toll of Drifting

Initially, aimlessness feels light, even liberating, but over time, a lack of purpose begins to take its toll and weigh heavily.

People who drift often experience:

- **Restlessness** - The nagging feeling that something is missing, but being unsure of what exactly.

- **Regret** - The sinking realisation that time is slipping away with little to show for it.

- **Comparison** - Watching others move forward and progress while feeling trapped in the same place.

- **Disconnection** - A persistent lack of fulfilment, even when everything appears "fine."

Eventually, drifting no longer feels like a choice; it feels like being lost.

Breaking Free: How to Start Moving Again

Drifting doesn't mean you're doomed to remain directionless. The key to shifting out of aimlessness is taking deliberate action - small, manageable steps that restore momentum.

1. Shrink the Decision

Instead of waiting for the opportunity to make one massive, life-changing choice, focus on the next *tiny* step.

Ask yourself:

☑ *What's one thing I can commit to today, just for now?*

☑ *What's one idea I can explore without overcommitting?*

☑ *What's a simple action that moves me forward, even slightly?*

A micro-move – writing for ten minutes, reaching out to someone new, signing up for a single class – generates movement, and movement breaks stagnation.

2. Move Without Perfection

Don't strive for perfect execution. Aim for progress.

Forward progress isn't about always making the right choice. It's about making *any* choice – then adjusting as you learn.

Perfection paralyzes action. Progress, even messy progress, beats waiting forever to start.

3. Anchor to a Bigger Why

Drifting often happens when we lack a meaningful anchor. Without a clear purpose, something that genuinely excites or challenges us, we float aimlessly through our days.

To create that anchor, ask yourself:

- ✅ *What kind of life do I want to build – not just today, but years from now?*

- ✅ *Who do I admire, and what about them resonates with me?*

- ✅ *What values do I want to live by?*

Clarity emerges from intention. When you give yourself something to aim for – even loosely – you weaken the pull of aimlessness.

4. Reroute the Fear of "Choosing Wrong"

One of the biggest myths about decision-making is that we need to make the right decisions every time, but in reality:

☑ Most decisions can be adjusted along the way.

☑ Very few choices lock you in permanently.

☑ Movement creates clarity that standing still never will.

Instead of worrying whether you are making the perfect decision, ask yourself, *"Will this decision move me forward in some way?"*

5. Create External Accountability

If you feel stuck, don't try to break the cycle alone. **External influences shift your mindset faster than internal thoughts alone ever will.**

Try:

☑ Telling someone about your goal, even casually mentioning it. A goal is harder to ignore if someone else knows about it.

☑ Joining a community that aligns with the direction you want to explore. Hearing how other people are doing can generate the energy you need to do the same.

☑ Setting up small, external commitments that nudge you toward action and celebrate each one as you achieve it.

When your environment supports movement, taking action feels natural.

Final Reflection: Movement Over Waiting

Drifting feels deceptive. It masquerades as freedom, but in truth, it's restraint in disguise.

The solution isn't forcing an immediate, dramatic change. It's breaking the stagnation, **even in the smallest way possible.**

So, if you feel stuck, don't wait for absolute clarity or certainty. Don't wait for the *perfect* next step.

Just move, because movement, however imperfect, pulls us out of stagnation and creates momentum.

2

The Obsession with Goals

How rigid focus narrows
our view and drains joy

"Success is a journey, not a destination."
ARTHUR ASHE

Goals can give us direction, a sense of purpose, and the thrill of chasing a dream. They serve as powerful motivators, inspiring us to reach higher, push harder, and measure our progress against clear benchmarks.

While it is important to avoid simply drifting through life, it is equally important not to lock ourselves into a purely goal-driven existence. When our focus on goals becomes rigid, we risk locking ourselves into tunnel vision that narrows our perspective and drains the joy from our daily lives. We end up trading the richness of the journey for an obsessive fixation on outcomes alone.

The Allure and the Pitfalls

There is little doubt that goal-setting offers clarity, structure and a direct path to success:

☑ CLARITY: Goals provide a clear target – a finish line to work toward.

☑ MOTIVATION: The prospect of achieving something tangible energizes us.

☑ ORDER: A set goal helps create a roadmap, offering control amid life's chaos.

However, this laser focus can come at a steep price:

☒ TUNNEL VISION: By zeroing in on a specific outcome, we become blind to the alternative opportunities and unexpected lessons our journey offers.

⊗ OPPRESSION AND EXHAUSTION: The relentless pressure to hit every milestone can drain our energy, dampen our creativity, and erode our well-being.

⊗ IDENTITY DESTRUCTION: When our self-worth becomes tied to reaching a predetermined target, each setback feels like personal failure rather than a chance to learn and grow.

What once motivated us becomes a source of stress – and sometimes, a creative block that paralyses our progress.

When Goals Become an Anchor Instead of a Compass

Imagine if every journey you took in life was through a tunnel from A to B. It might be an efficient way to travel, but it would also be very limiting. You might reach your destination, but you would miss all of the scenery on either side of your path. What if the real opportunity lay in the detours and unexpected landscapes outside of that tunnel?

When we obsess over predetermined goals, we risk:

⊗ MISSING LIFE'S DETAILS: In our single-minded pursuit, we can overlook the small, serendipitous moments that give life meaning.

⊗ NEGLECTING FLEXIBILITY: The natural world isn't rigid – a tree grows toward the light, yet bends with every gust of wind. Our paths shouldn't be inflexible either. We thrive not by forcing ourselves down one exact route, but by adapting and flowing as circumstances shift around us.

⊗ EXPERIENCING BURNOUT: The relentless pressure to achieve creates exhaustion and a sense of dissatisfaction, even when we hit our targets. The journey is transformed from enrichment and growth into mechanically checking boxes on an endless list.

Rigid focus narrows our vision dramatically. It reduces vibrant landscapes to mere backdrops for our relentless pursuit of success, leaving us drained and cut off from the wonder that surrounds us daily.

Case Study: Jake's Awakening

Jake embodied goal obsession. Every morning, he methodically checked off tasks from his carefully planned schedule, convinced that only laser focus would drive his start-up to success. For months, he pursued every target with tunnel vision. Despite achieving impressive external milestones, he felt increasingly hollow and exhausted. Meetings became robotic, ideas felt stale, and even victories passed without celebration. They were simply ticks in boxes.

Jake received a message from a friend inviting him to join her and another friend for a coffee. Jake declined – his schedule was set. His focus was locked on securing funding for his next project, and he had no time for speculative meetings or opportunistic networking that week.

Jake later discovered that the unknown individual had just sold their technology business and was looking for investment opportunities. The combination of expertise and finance they brought to the table could have been a springboard for Jake's own business. This loss jolted him awake – his narrow focus had blinded him to valuable, unexpected possibilities.

Determined to rediscover his lost passion, he started scheduling regular reflection time, celebrating small wins, and building flexibility into his plans. Gradually, Jake found that embracing a more adaptable, process-focused approach not only rekindled his creativity but also delivered more sustainable, well-rounded success.

● ● ●

The Emotional and Psychological Trade-Offs

When goals consume everything, performance pressure distorts our relationship with work and can create negative impacts such as:

- ⊗ STIFLED CREATIVITY: Fear of straying from the "right" path paralyses innovation, crushing opportunities to experiment and learn from setbacks.

- ⊗ ERODED JOY: The thrill of progress slowly transforms into anxiety over every small mistake, turning the journey into a sterile checklist instead of meaningful experiences.

- ⊗ FIXED MINDSET: Rigid focus kills adaptability, making it nearly impossible to reassess and adapt when circumstances shift or fresh opportunities emerge.

Practical Work Plan: Reclaiming Balance and Joy

To counteract the potentially draining impact of focusing solely on rigid goals, consider this actionable plan:

☑ REFLECT ON YOUR CURRENT FOCUS:

  ☑ JOURNAL SESSION: Write down your top three goals. Next to each one, list one positive outcome you expect and one potential drawback of focusing solely on that outcome.

  ☑ SELF-ASSESSMENT: Ask yourself, "Am I too focused on the destination? What happiness, learning or opportunities might I be missing along the way?"

☑ SET MICRO-MOVES INSTEAD OF MONUMENTAL MILESTONES:

  ☑ BREAK IT DOWN: Divide each major goal into smaller, manageable tasks. For example, rather than aiming to "launch a new product," start with "research market trends for 15 minutes each day."

  ☑ CELEBRATE SMALL WINS: Create a rewards system for achieving these micro-goals. Each milestone becomes a reason to pause, reflect, and enjoy your progress.

☑ CREATE FLEXIBILITY IN YOUR PLANNING:

  ☑ WEEKLY CHECK-IN: Dedicate 20 minutes every week to evaluate your goals. Ask: "What unexpected opportunities arose this week? How can I weave these into my plan?"

- ☑ ADJUST YOUR COURSE: When you notice signs of burnout or diminishing happiness, adjust your goals. It's perfectly okay to recalibrate your direction based on new insights.

☑ PRACTICE MINDFULNESS AND PRESENCE:

- ☑ DAILY MEDITATION: Spend 5-10 minutes in meditation or mindful breathing to anchor yourself in the present. This practice helps break the cycle of obsessive future focus.

- ☑ GRATITUDE JOURNALING: Each day, note one thing you enjoyed about the process, not just the end result.

☑ BUILD AN ACCOUNTABILITY BUDDY SYSTEM:

- ☑ PARTNER UP: Find a colleague, friend, or mentor who values both achievement and well-being. Share your progress and challenges while mutually encouraging each other to remain flexible and joyful.

- ☑ REGULAR FEEDBACK: Schedule bi-weekly meetings to review not only your successes but also your learning moments and surprises encountered along the way.

🐑 🐑 🐑

Final Reflection: Balancing Ambition with Adaptability

A strong focus on goals can drive us to great heights, but when that focus becomes rigid, it can also narrow our perspective and drain happiness from our lives. The key lies not in abandoning our ambitions, but in balancing them with the flexibility to adapt, reflect, and savour the journey. By reframing goals as a dynamic compass rather than a fixed destination, we open ourselves to growth, unexpected opportunities, and the vibrant joys of everyday progress.

Remember, every step you take – even those that seem small or those that aren't perfectly planned – brings you closer to a life that's both successful and profoundly fulfilling. Embrace the micro-moves, celebrate the journey, and allow your path to evolve naturally along the way.

3

When Force Fails

The burnout cycle and why "try harder" isn't always the solution

"Sometimes pushing harder is exactly what holds you back — learn to flow, not force."

UNKNOWN

We've all heard the mantra: "Just try harder."

In a culture that champions relentless drive, the idea that sheer willpower can overcome any obstacle seems not only heroic but essential. Yet the reality is that pushing yourself beyond natural limits often leads not to breakthrough success but to the burnout cycle. A state where your energy depletes, creativity stifles, and joy evaporates.

The Burnout Cycle: A Vicious Circle

When we rely solely on force, on sheer persistence without pause, we set ourselves on a path toward exhaustion.

⊗ OVEREXERTION: Constantly trying to push through challenges creates an energy deficit. When you force your way through problems, the relentless pressure eventually wears you down.

⊗ DIMINISHED RETURNS: At first, extra effort might yield progress. But as fatigue sets in, each additional push contributes less to your goal while taking a heavier toll on your wellbeing.

⊗ EMOTIONAL DEPLETION: The "try harder" mindset sends the message that rest equals weakness. Over time, this lack of balance between work and restorative downtime leads to increased stress, anxiety, and even depression.

In this cycle, the more you force, the less effective your efforts become. Rather than overcoming obstacles, you find yourself battling recurring fatigue, frustration, and a persistent sense of failure despite your best intentions.

The Limits of Force: When Pushing Backfires

Consider Alex, a driven professional who believed that endless hours and relentless effort would guarantee his success. For months, Alex doubled his workload and sacrificed sleep, convinced that every extra minute of grinding would bring him closer to his dream promotion. However, as weeks turned into months, Alex began experiencing crushing burnout. Meetings blurred together, his creativity dried up, and even his passion for the work he once loved began to disappear. Eventually, Alex's body and mind simply refused to maintain the pace. He crashed, unable to motivate himself to get out of bed, let alone drive his business forward. The very push he thought was necessary ended up sabotaging his long-term goals, forcing him to completely rethink his approach.

Alex took a holiday and spent two weeks recharging his batteries. On his return, he created a new manifesto for his work and life which included regular downtime and daily reflection. His business growth slowed a little, but his clarity of mind and overall energy soared. He found he found he was making better decisions and not only enjoying work again but enjoying life outside of work too.

Alex's story isn't unique, but he was one of the lucky ones who managed to make it through to the other side. Many of us discover that when we try to force our way through life, we unknowingly trade short-term progress for lasting damage. All too often, not only does the constant pressure to "try harder" make us blind to more sustainable, creative, and flexible ways to solve problems, we don't see these signs until it is too late.

Rethinking "Try Harder": Embracing a New Paradigm

The mistake isn't having goals or ambitions – it's believing that brute force is the only path forward. Sometimes, the answer isn't pushing harder but stepping back, recalibrating, and embracing a more adaptive strategy.

Nature's Example

Look at the natural world. Trees that resist every gust of wind without bending are the ones most likely to snap. Those that sway, absorb nature's force without being destroyed by it.

- ✅ ADAPTABILITY OVER RIGIDITY: Flexibility lets you absorb shocks, pivot when necessary, and maintain momentum even when conditions shift.

- ✅ MINDFUL REST: Knowing when to pause isn't failure – it's a crucial strategy for recharging your creativity and resilience.

Rather than clinging to the "try harder" mindset, consider adopting a "work smarter by flowing with life" approach. This doesn't mean abandoning your ambitions – it means respecting your natural limits, learning from setbacks, and allowing for growth that isn't powered solely by strain.

Practical Work Plan: Breaking the Burnout Cycle

To move away from the exhausting force-driven approach, try this actionable plan:

- ☑ RECOGNIZE YOUR LIMITS:

  - ☑ SELF-CHECK EXERCISE: At the end of each day, rate your energy and stress levels on a scale from 1 to 10. Look for patterns in which pushing yourself too hard consistently leads to lower scores.

  - ☑ BODY AWARENESS: Pay attention to physical signals like muscle tension, fatigue, or headaches – these are your body's way of telling you to ease up.

- ☑ REDEFINE SUCCESS:

  - ☑ VALUE THE PROCESS: Write a brief reflection on why you chose your current path. What parts of the journey genuinely bring you joy? Make it a habit to celebrate small victories, not just major achievements.

  - ☑ REFRAME FAILURE: Replace thoughts like "I failed because I didn't try hard enough" with "This setback gives me valuable information to adjust my approach and grow."

- ☑ INTEGRATE REST AND RECOVERY:

  - ☑ SCHEDULED PAUSES: Build regular breaks and downtime into your schedule. Try a 10-minute mindfulness break every two hours or dedicate one full rest day each week.

  - ☑ MINDFULNESS PRACTICE: Start with just 5-10 minutes of meditation or deep breathing daily. Extend this time as you become more in tune with what your body needs.

- ☑ ADOPT A FLEXIBLE MINDSET:

  - ☑ SET ADAPTIVE GOALS: Rather than rigid targets, create flexible milestones that leave room for adjustments. Ask yourself weekly, "How can I tweak my approach to keep making progress without burning out?"

  - ☑ FEEDBACK LOOPS: Keep a simple journal where you note what worked, what didn't, and what new possibilities opened up when you allowed yourself to change course.

- ☑ SEEK SUPPORT:

  - ☑ ACCOUNTABILITY PARTNERS: Connect with someone who understands the dangers of burnout. Regular check-ins help you stay accountable without falling back into the overexertion trap.

✓ PROFESSIONAL GUIDANCE: A mentor, coach, or therapist can provide a fresh perspective on how to balance your drive with genuine self-care.

🌼 🌼 🌼

💨 Final Reflection: When Force Fails, Flow Prevails

In our relentless pursuit of success, we easily fall into the trap that more force automatically means more progress, but the burnout cycle shows us there's a point where "try harder" must give way to "try smarter." When you listen to your body, respect your limits, and embrace flexible adaptation, you create room for lasting progress and rediscover the joy in your work.

The most resilient people aren't those who simply bulldoze through their challenges – they're those who learn to flow with life, adapting gracefully to its natural rhythms. When you choose to bend rather than break, you tap into the true power of your inner strength and creativity.

So, the next time you feel the urge to force your way through a challenge, pause, think back to Alex's story, tune into your inner signals, and ask yourself: *Is there a gentler way forward – one that honours both my ambitions and my well-being?* Embrace the idea that sometimes, the most effective strategy is to release the need for force and instead trust life's natural flow to guide you.

💨 💨 💨

4

Bending with the Breeze – The Art of Flexible Focus

Why nature bends, and how we can too

"When the winds of change blow, bend your branches; rigid trees do not survive the storm"

ANONYMOUS

Step outside on a windy day and watch the willow trees dance gracefully with the breeze. It's impossible not to feel inspired by nature's effortless adaptation. In every swaying branch, every root that curves around a stone, nature reveals a profound truth: real strength doesn't come from rigid resistance but from the ability to adjust, flex, and discover new paths when the old ones become blocked.

In our fast-paced world, we're constantly told to stand firm, to lock onto our goals with laser focus and push forward no matter what stands in our way. Yet this "all-or-nothing" approach often leads to frustration, burnout, and missed opportunities. Flexible focus offers a different way: holding onto your purpose with a light touch, creating space to innovate, adapt, and, most importantly, actually enjoy the journey.

The Lessons Nature Teaches Us

1. The Bending Tree: Strength in Surrender

Picture a mighty oak standing beside a graceful willow. The oak, despite its impressive strength, often snaps under a heavy storm's pressure because it refuses to yield. The willow, however, bends with the wind. Its branches don't battle the storm; they yield gracefully and spring back once the force passes. This isn't weakness; it's a masterful act of resilience.

The willow teaches us that sometimes, the wisest way to face adversity isn't through brute force confrontation, but by embracing the flexibility to adapt. When you bend with the breeze, you absorb life's challenges and then spring back with renewed strength. It's about conserving energy, not wasting it fighting what you can't control, but channelling it toward growth and renewal instead.

2. The Wandering Roots: Redirection as Progress

Beneath the surface, roots encounter real obstacles - rocks, compacted soil, and buried debris. A plant's instinct isn't to stop growing but to find another way forward. These roots spread sideways, dig deeper, and eventually discover vital nutrients around the obstruction. This redirection becomes the plant's path to thriving despite the barriers.

When we hit roadblocks in life, our first instinct often pushes us to force our way through. But like those wandering roots, a smarter approach involves pausing to search for alternate pathways around the obstacles. This redirection frequently unveils opportunities that bulldozing straight ahead would have missed entirely.

3. The Flowing Water: Embracing Fluidity

Water embodies perfect flexibility. It shapes itself to any container, seeks the path of least resistance, and gradually erodes even the hardest stone. Water's adaptability isn't surrender - it's persistent determination. Through constant movement and adjustment, water carves canyons and nurtures entire ecosystems.

When you adopt water's mindset in your own life, you learn to flow gracefully through uncertainty, adjust when needed, and transform obstacles into stepping stones for continuous growth.

The Philosophy of Flexible Focus

Flexible focus means pursuing your intentions and goals without becoming so locked into one rigid method that you miss the changing landscape around you. It's the sweet spot between ambition and mindfulness - a dynamic dance of planning and spontaneity.

The Pitfalls of Rigid Focus

Reflect for a moment on the learnings of chapter 2 and remember the issues that a rigid focus on goals can bring.

- ⊗ TUNNEL VISION: When you fixate solely on one outcome, you miss the subtle signals and unexpected opportunities that appear along the way.

- ⊗ EXHAUSTION: Relentlessly forcing success drains your energy, creativity, and joy.

- ⊗ RESISTANCE TO CHANGE: An overly fixed approach leaves no room for adaptation when unexpected challenges emerge.

Embracing a Flexible Mindset

Now consider how adapting a more flexible mindset can result in a much healthier and more successful environment.

☑ ADAPTATION OVER DEFIANCE: Understand that adapting to circumstances doesn't mean surrendering your dreams – it means evolving alongside them.

☑ LIVING IN THE PRESENT: Allow yourself to stay present and mindful, noticing the beauty in your journey rather than fixating solely on a distant destination.

☑ CONTINUOUS RECALIBRATION: Regular reflection and adjustment help you maintain aligned focus without the stress that comes with rigidity.

Case Study: Sarah's Journey to Flexible Focus

Sarah was a high-performing marketing executive with a string of successes she'd relentlessly pursued through rigid routines and painstaking attention to detail. For years, her life resembled a checklist of goals: hit quarterly targets, secure new accounts, expand her team. Yet, despite her accomplishments, Sarah found herself increasingly exhausted and disconnected from the joy of her work.

During a particularly stressful period, Sarah missed a crucial opportunity – a chance encounter with a former colleague who had fresh insights and innovative ideas that could have revolutionized her approach. It wasn't that Sarah didn't care; she was so narrowly focused on her carefully charted path that she'd traded spontaneity for certainty.

After recognizing this pattern, Sarah began experimenting with small adjustments. She scheduled regular "flex-breaks" throughout her day - brief mindfulness exercises, casual conversations with colleagues, and walks outdoors. Over time, these small moments of flexibility transformed her entire work strategy. Her creativity resurged, her energy returned, and her approach became more holistic and adaptable. Sarah discovered that by bending with the breeze of change, she could not only achieve her goals but also enjoy the journey of getting there.

● ● ●

Practical Work Plan for Cultivating Flexible Focus

To help integrate the art of bending with the breeze into your daily life, follow this practical work plan:

Step 1: Daily Reflection and Mindfulness

☑ MORNING CHECK-IN: Start your day with a 5-minute mindfulness or meditation session. Focus on your breath and let yourself be present. Ask, "What energy do I want to carry into today?"

☑ VISUAL PROMPTS: Place a small object (like a smooth stone or miniature willow figurine) on your desk as a reminder to stay flexible.

Step 2: Adaptive Goal Setting

☑ BREAK DOWN GOALS: Instead of pursuing one massive target, divide your goals into smaller steps that allow room

for adjustment. Write down your primary goal and list
flexible actions you can take daily.

☑ WEEKLY REVIEW: At the end of each week, reflect on what
worked and what didn't. Adjust your micro-move plan
accordingly, treating yourself with compassion rather than
judgment.

Step 3: Embrace Redirection through Journaling

☑ OBSTACLE MAPPING: Keep a journal to document any
challenges you face. For each obstacle, brainstorm at least
three alternative approaches to the situation.

☑ GRATITUDE AND GROWTH: Write about a time when
an unexpected turn led to growth or joy. Remember that
setbacks often clear the path for innovation and new
possibilities.

Step 4: Incorporate Movement and Nature

☑ NATURE WALKS: Set aside time each week to spend
outdoors, watching how nature adapts and shifts with the
breeze. Consider how these natural rhythms might apply to
your personal and professional challenges.

☑ MINDFUL MOVEMENT: Practice activities that encourage
fluidity and presence – yoga, tai chi, or even dancing in your
living room. Let your body show you the beauty of moving
with flexibility rather than rigidity.

Step 5: Seek Feedback and Build Community

☑ ACCOUNTABILITY PARTNERSHIPS: Partner with someone who shares your commitment to flexible living. Check in regularly, exchanging insights and supporting each other through life's inevitable changes.

☑ GROUP REFLECTION SESSIONS: Join or start a group focused on discussing challenges and creative solutions. Fresh perspectives from others can completely reshape how you approach your own obstacles.

🌳 🌳 🌳

🍃 Final Reflection: The Power of Bending

Bending with the breeze doesn't mean abandoning your dreams or surrendering your goals, it means cultivating an adaptive mindset that honours both your aspirations and your well-being. When you view obstacles as invitations for redirection, you create space for a more resilient, creative, and joyful path forward.

Remember, you're not a rigid structure waiting to snap under pressure. You're a dynamic being with the natural ability to flow, recalibrate, and flourish amid change. Like the willow tree, let your strength show not in how firmly you resist the wind, but in how gracefully you dance with it.

As you continue forward, let nature's gentle wisdom guide your steps. When life sends a storm your way, pause, breathe deeply, and bend with the breeze. In that graceful movement lies the essence of flexible focus – your gateway to lasting progress and deep fulfilment.

At the end of this book is a practical worksheet designed to help you actively apply and internalise the principles of flexible focus discussed in this chapter. Use this worksheet daily or weekly to reflect on your progress, identify opportunities to adapt, and build resilience through mindful redirection.

🌬 🌬 🌬

5

The Detour Is Not the End

Learning to pivot with purpose
when life redirects you

*"Life's setbacks are not dead ends but
stepping stones — each detour guides us toward
paths we might never have discovered."*

ANONYMOUS

We often think of our plans as straight lines - careers, relationships, ambitions - each step calculated to reach a predetermined destination. Yet life rarely follows our carefully drawn maps. Unexpected detours - job losses, relationship shifts, health challenges, or global events - appear without warning, forcing us off our intended course. Instead of viewing these detours as failures or dead ends, we can learn to see them as opportunities for redirection, growth, and renewal.

The Nature of Detours

A detour is simply a temporary change in route, not a signal that the journey must end. When roads close, we learn to navigate side streets. Similarly, when life's "road closures" appear, our ability to pivot with intention determines whether we remain stuck or continue moving forward.

Why Detours Happen

- ☑ EXTERNAL CIRCUMSTANCES: Economic downturns, industry shifts, or a pandemic can make our original plans impossible to pursue.

- ☑ INTERNAL AWAKENING: Sometimes our priorities evolve - values shift, passions change, or a quiet voice inside insists that the path we're on no longer aligns with who we've become.

☑ UNFORESEEN EVENTS: Accidents, illness, or sudden loss can reroute our lives in an instant, demanding adaptation we neither expected nor wanted.

In each case, the detour feels jarring. We grip the steering wheel of our plans, resisting the change. But just as a river bends around a boulder, we can learn to flow around life's obstacles and carry our momentum in a new direction.

The Psychology of Redirecting

When we face a sudden redirection, our initial reaction often involves resistance: denial, frustration, or grief for what we've lost. These reactions are natural, but if we let them fester, they trap us in stagnation. Instead, embracing the emotional process paves the way to purposeful pivoting.

☑ ACKNOWLEDGING THE LOSS

☑ FEEL THE EMOTIONS: Whether it's disappointment over a lost job, sadness over a relationship ending, or fear of an uncertain future, allow yourself to experience these emotions fully.

☑ NAME THE DETOUR: Clearly state what has changed. "My project was cancelled" or "Our move fell through" grounds you in reality rather than letting vague anxiety linger.

✅ REFRAMING THE NARRATIVE

✅ FROM BLOCKAGE TO REDIRECTION: Instead of labelling the detour as a "failure," call it a "course correction." This shift in language reframes your perspective and opens new possibilities.

✅ SEE THE SILVER LININGS: Ask yourself, "What might this change reveal that I couldn't see before?" Even if the answer isn't immediately clear, planting the seed of possibility allows creativity to take root.

✅ CULTIVATING A GROWTH MINDSET

✅ EMBRACE LEARNING OVER PERFECTION: Understand that detours teach valuable lessons – resilience, adaptability, and self-discovery. Rather than viewing yourself as off-track, see yourself as in training.

✅ CELEBRATE SMALL WINS: Every step you take toward understanding or exploring a new direction – researching a new field, reconnecting with a supportive friend, or simply sending out one application – deserves recognition.

Case Study: Marcus's Unexpected Pivot

Marcus had spent seven years climbing the corporate ladder at a tech firm. He took pride in his role as a product manager and had mapped out clear milestones – promotion to director, a sizable bonus each year, and a comfortable salary. When his company announced an unexpected restructuring, Marcus found himself laid off. Shock turned into panic as he grappled with his financial obligations and the identity crisis that followed: "Who am I without this title?"

After a week of numbness, Marcus reached out to a former colleague who had transitioned into freelance consulting. Over coffee, he discovered the freedom (and the challenges) of working independently. Back home, Marcus allowed himself to grieve the stability he had lost, then began asking a different question: "What skills have I developed in product management that I can repurpose?"

He recognized his strengths in market research, cross-functional communication, and agile project execution. Within days, he drafted a plan to offer freelance product strategy sessions to early-stage startups. He invested time updating his social media profiles, attending virtual networking events, and crafting a simple website.

Six months later, Marcus had three regular clients, a flexible schedule, and the excitement of shaping products from the ground up. The detour that initially felt catastrophic had redirected him to a career path that offered both autonomy and alignment with his values.

※ ※ ※

The Pillars of Purposeful Pivoting

When life redirects you, how you respond determines whether the detour becomes a dead end or a pathway to something equally - or even more - fulfilling. These pillars will help you pivot with clear intention:

☑ CLARIFY YOUR CORE VALUES

    ☑ VALUES INVENTORY: List the top five values guiding your choices - integrity, creativity, autonomy, service, or growth, for example. When your career or circumstances change, measure new opportunities against this inventory.

    ☑ ALIGN OVER ACHIEVE: Instead of chasing a title or a pay cheque, focus on roles and projects that resonate with your values. This alignment ensures each pivot moves you closer to long-term fulfilment.

☑ LEVERAGE TRANSFERABLE STRENGTHS

    ☑ SKILL MAPPING: Write down every skill you've honed in your current or previous roles - communication, problem-solving, empathy, or technical know-how. Next to each, list industries or functions where that skill adds value.

    ☑ BRIDGE BUILDING: Identify one way to connect with a professional in that adjacent field - send a LinkedIn message, schedule an informational interview, or attend a themed webinar. Every conversation deepens your understanding of how to apply your strengths in new contexts.

- ✅ EXPERIMENT AND ITERATE

  - ✅ SMALL-SCALE EXPERIMENTS: Rather than diving in headfirst, test new directions with minimal risk. Offer pro bono consulting for a nonprofit, take an online course, or volunteer in a community project that aligns with your interests.

  - ✅ FEEDBACK LOOPS: After each experiment, journal what you learned: Did it energize or drain you? Did it match your expectations? Use these insights to refine your next step.

- ✅ BUILD A SUPPORTIVE ECOSYSTEM

  - ✅ MENTORS AND PEERS: Seek mentors who have navigated similar detours. Their wisdom can save you time and emotional distress. Join peer groups, online or in person, filled with people exploring parallel pivots. Mutual encouragement fuels momentum.

  - ✅ ACCOUNTABILITY STRUCTURES: Set up regular check-ins with a trusted friend, coach, or mentor. Share your goals, timeline, and stumbling blocks. External accountability keeps you on course when self-doubt creeps in.

- ✅ MAINTAIN EMOTIONAL RESILIENCE

  - ✅ MINDFUL PRACTICES: Daily meditation, journaling, or a simple five-minute breathing break can ground you when uncertainty threatens to overwhelm. These practices build resilience, helping you approach detours with a calm, curious mindset rather than panic.

- ☑ CELEBRATE PROGRESS, NOT PERFECTION: Each detour step you take such as sending one email, drafting a mini-plan, or attending a networking event, represents progress. Reward these small victories to reinforce your sense of agency.

Practical Work Plan: Navigating Your Detour with Intention

Use this step-by-step guide the next time life's unpredictable currents push you off your planned course:

1. Acknowledge and Accept

- ☑ Take one uninterrupted hour to sit with your feelings: disappointment, fear, or anger. Write them down without judgment.

- ☑ Name the detour explicitly: "My startup didn't receive funding," or "My partner and I are going separate ways."

2. Reframe and Redefine

- ☑ Write a brief reflection: "If this detour is redirecting me, where might I be headed instead?"

☑ Brainstorm three positive reframes – for example, "I now have time to explore my passion for writing," or "This role change opens doors to a more fulfilling industry."

3. Values and Strengths Alignment

☑ Create a "Values and Skills Matrix." In one column, list your top five values. In another, list your five strongest transferable skills.

☑ Draw arrows connecting values with skills – like "Autonomy ⟷ Project Management" or "Service ⟷ Client Communication."

4. Generate Pivot Options

☑ Set a 20-minute timer and brainstorm five alternative directions that honour your values and use your skills.

☑ Don't hold back – every idea counts. After brainstorming, underline the two options that excite you most.

5. Design a Micro-Experiment for Each Option

☑ For each of your two chosen options, create a micro-experiment you can finish within two weeks. Examples:

- Reach out to three professionals in your target field to see if they might be open for an informal chat.

- Enrol in a short online workshop to test your interest and natural ability.

- Volunteer one afternoon per week to dip your toes into a new role or industry.

6. Reflect and Iterate

☑ After completing each micro-experiment, answer these questions in your journal:

- What energized me?

- What felt draining?

- What did I discover about myself and this potential path?

☑ Use these insights to decide which option deserves deeper exploration and what tweaks to make.

7. Seek Support and Accountability

☑ Find one mentor or peer group to join. Schedule your first meeting or call within the next week. Share your micro-experiment results and ask for feedback or connections.

8. Commit to a 30-Day Pivot Plan

☑ Map out three specific actions you'll take in the next 30 days toward your chosen direction: update your resume, attend a virtual industry meetup, or draft your first proposal. Block time for these actions on your calendar with firm dates.

9. Celebrate Milestones

☑ After each completed action, pause to recognise your courage and progress. Share the milestone with a trusted friend or post it in a supportive community.

🌀 🌀 🌀

🍃 Final Reflection: Embracing the Detour's Gift

When life reroutes us, it's tempting to mourn the loss of our original plan. Yet detours are rarely random; they often signal that the life we envisioned no longer matches who we're becoming. Just as a GPS recalculates when we miss an exit, our inner compass guides us toward a path that better aligns with our evolving values, strengths, and purpose.

Remember:

☑ A DETOUR IS NOT A DEAD END. It's an invitation to explore landscapes we might never have discovered otherwise.

☑ YOUR ABILITY TO PIVOT WITH PURPOSE STARTS WITH ACCEPTANCE. Feel your emotions fully, then reframe the detour as a necessary course correction.

☑ CLARITY EMERGES THROUGH SMALL EXPERIMENTS. Test ideas, learn from results, and iterate rather than waiting for the perfect solution to appear.

☑ SEEK CONNECTION. The wisdom of mentors and peers can illuminate possibilities you can't see on your own.

⊘ VALUE THE JOURNEY AS MUCH AS THE DESTINATION.
Each step of your detour contributes to your story of
resilience and reinvention.

No matter how unexpected the redirection, remember that
you hold the pen to your narrative. By pivoting with intention,
you transform detours into new beginnings - opening vistas of
possibility that ultimately bring you closer to a life of deeper
purpose and fulfilment.

⇝ ⇝ ⇝

6

Nature's Teachers – What Roots, Trees, and Wind Reveal

Biological metaphors that teach thriving through change

"In every walk with nature,
one receives far more than he seeks."
JOHN MUIR

In our quest for progress, we often forget we're part of a living world that has been mastering change and resilience for billions of years. Nature isn't just a backdrop to our ambitions - it's a mentor. One that never yells, but always teaches.

While we turn to apps, schedules, and productivity hacks for guidance, some of the deepest wisdom about thriving in uncertain times is right outside your window. The trees, the soil, the rivers, and the air - they've been bending, shifting, adapting, and growing long before humans ever created a word for "resilience."

Perhaps it is time to stop pushing, stop resisting, and start listening.

Lesson 1: Roots – Quiet Tenacity and Intelligent Rerouting

You'll never hear roots grow. But you'll feel their impact in the strength of the tallest trees.

Beneath every flourishing plant is a silent, steady network that adapts relentlessly. When a root hits concrete or stone, it doesn't give up. It doesn't dig harder in frustration. It simply adjusts. It finds another path, moves around the obstacle, and keeps seeking water and nutrients.

What this teaches us:

☑ Obstacles are not barriers - they're redirections.

☑ Progress doesn't have to be loud to be powerful.

☑ If one path closes, growth is still possible in another direction.

Practical Reflection:

Think of a challenge you're currently facing. What if, like a root, you stopped trying to bulldoze through it – and instead asked, "Where else could I grow?"

Lesson 2: Trees – Strength in Swaying

We admire tall trees for their grandeur, but it's their flexibility that keeps them standing.

During hurricanes and high winds, rigid trees often snap. But trees like willows, palms, and even oaks survive by bending. Their branches give way temporarily, trusting that the storm will pass and their roots will hold.

This balance between yielding and anchoring is the secret to long-term resilience

What this teaches us:

☑ Flexibility is not weakness – it's survival.

☑ Deep grounding allows for temporary movement.

☑ What bends today can rise again tomorrow.

Mind-Body Integration:

Next time you feel overwhelmed or emotionally "hit" by a situation, try this:

☑ Pause and close your eyes.

☑ Inhale deeply and exhale slowly.

☑ Imagine your emotions as wind, and your body as a tree. Can you sway without snapping?

Lesson 3: Wind – Invisible Influence and Relentless Movement

You can't see the wind, but it shapes everything it touches.

It sculpts sand dunes, moves clouds, and carries seeds across vast distances. It doesn't ask permission. It doesn't have a fixed direction. It just moves - persistently, invisibly, and often unpredictably.

Wind reminds us that influence doesn't have to be loud. That progress can happen without force. That change is constant and often unseen until much later.

What this teaches us:

☑ Not all transformation is visible.

☑ Small shifts create long-term change.

☑ Trusting unseen forces - intuition, emotion, timing - can be powerful.

Case Study: Amelia's Quiet Shift

After a difficult breakup and job burnout, Amelia tried everything - therapy, new routines, a move to another city. But nothing "worked" immediately. Then she started walking every morning, watching the wind move the trees. Slowly, without drama, she felt herself loosening. Letting go. Her life wasn't fixed, but she was no longer stuck. She imagined the breeze blowing through her head, taking with it the self-limiting thoughts and ideas she had unwittingly held on to for years. She allowed her mind to empty and slowly refill itself with new thoughts. She considered each thought as it arose, and if she felt it wasn't of use to her at that time, she let it go again, knowing that it would return when the time was right. The thoughts she did hang on to, she carefully planted in her mind and nurtured them, allowing them the freedom to grow and flourish into whatever they needed to become.

Over time, she found that she had let go of the past and was focusing on the future. Not in a rigid sense, but as a destination in which she knew she would flourish and be happy.

Sometimes, the healing happens so quietly, you don't notice it until you've already grown.

● ● ●

Lesson 4: Fire – Transformation Through Tension

Fire often gets a bad rap - it burns, destroys, consumes. But fire also clears what no longer serves. It makes space for renewal.

In many forests, fire is part of the ecosystem. Certain seeds can only sprout after a blaze. Old growth is cleared to make room for new life.

What this teaches us:

☑ Destruction can lead to rebirth.

☑ Sometimes what feels like failure is clearing space.

☑ Transformation often begins in discomfort.

Exercise: Release and Renewal

Write down one habit, belief, or commitment that feels heavy or outdated. Then symbolically "burn" it - tear the paper, or simply say aloud, "This no longer serves me." Then write one small action that supports your next season of growth.

Nature's Cycles – Accepting the Seasons of Life

Nature doesn't bloom year-round. Trees lose their leaves. Bears hibernate. Fields lay fallow.

Why then, do we expect ourselves to be endlessly productive?

Rest is not laziness. Stillness is not failure. Winter is not death - it's preparation for spring.

Seasonal Self-Check-In:

Ask yourself:

- ✅ Am I in a season of planting, growth, harvest, or rest?

- ✅ What does my current "season" need from me?

- ✅ What can I let go of so I can nourish the next phase?

Final Reflection: Let Nature Lead You Home

Nature doesn't rush, yet everything gets done. Trees don't grow faster because of anxiety. Rivers don't panic when the landscape changes. Roots don't resist redirection, they simply adapt. And yet, somehow, everything in nature flourishes.

What if you did the same?

The lessons of roots, trees, and wind aren't just poetic metaphors. They're ancient blueprints for modern resilience. You are not separate from nature - you are an extension of it. You were built to adapt, to sway with stress, to grow through challenge, and to trust invisible forces to guide your next step.

When life feels overwhelming, ask yourself, "Am I trying to force something that wants to flow? Am I standing rigid when the moment is asking me to bend?"

Remember, your power is not in how tightly you grip your plans, but in how gracefully you respond to the unexpected.

Let your life mirror the quiet wisdom of the earth - deeply rooted, openly flexible, and always moving toward growth.

Let nature lead you home.

You don't need to control everything to be okay. You don't need to know the entire path to keep growing.

Like the root, you'll find another way.

Like the tree, you'll rise again.

Like the wind, you'll move with unseen strength.

Like the fire, you'll let go of what must burn so something new can begin.

And in the quiet rhythms of the earth, you'll remember: you are not broken.

You are becoming.

7

Purpose Over Plan

Redefining success by
anchoring to values,
not rigid outcomes

*"He who has a **why** to live for can bear
almost any **how**."*
FRIEDRICH NIETZSCHE

When life shifts unexpectedly, plans crumble, and the path ahead grows murky, one thing must remain steady: your purpose.

Purpose isn't a goal. It's not a job title or a five-year plan. It's not even a passion. Purpose is your compass – the deep, underlying reason why you do what you do, why you move, strive, care, and keep going.

Your goals are what you want to achieve.

Your identity is who you want to be.

Your purpose is why you want to achieve those things and why you want to be that person.

While goals may shift, identity may evolve, but purpose endures.

Levels of Purpose

Purpose operates at every level of human life. At the deepest level, we talk about a purpose in life. This is a level of purpose that few of us will ever really consider, but centres around the question of *why* we are here. For most of us this is a question which is simply too big for us to consider and so, we avoid the question of purpose altogether.

However, the question of purpose can be just as valid and powerful at many other levers.

For example, we might consider our purpose at work. Do we work simply to earn a salary in order to pay the bills, or is there some deeper purpose we can attribute to our job? As a scientist, it may be to find a cure for a disease. As a teacher, it may be to inspire a generation of children. As a barista, it may be to make the best cup of coffee that every customer has ever tasted.

At an even more focused level, we might consider our purpose in the moment.

For example, when arguing with a friend, is our purpose in that moment to vent our anger or is it to help them see there is another option, a better option, an opportunity to make a choice which will benefit them?

Why Purpose Matters More Than Plans

We often confuse clarity of plan with clarity of purpose. But they're fundamentally different.

Plans are tactical. They show you how to get from A to B.

Purpose is strategic. It reveals *why* you want to reach B in the first place.

When you anchor yourself to a purpose:

✅ You become less reactive to change.

✅ You recover faster after setbacks.

✅ You're less likely to quit when one path closes.

By considering and understanding your purpose in every moment, you will develop a better understanding of why you do what you do. As this becomes clear in your mind, you will begin to make better choices about who you want to be and how you will become that person.

The Problem with Performance-Based Identity

Many people tie their identity to achievement. They wrap their worth around what they accomplish. So, when something fails – when a launch flops, a relationship ends, a job disappears – it's not just a plan that dies. A piece of *them* dies with it.

That's why anchoring in **purpose** is vital.

When your identity is grounded in *why* you exist – not *what* you produce – you're no longer at the mercy of external events. You become internally guided, not externally defined.

Discovering Your North Star

Finding your purpose isn't about waiting for lightning to strike. It's about asking better questions.

- ☑ What gives me energy – even when I'm tired?
- ☑ What am I willing to struggle for?
- ☑ Who or what do I feel naturally called to serve?
- ☑ What patterns keep showing up in my life?
- ☑ If success and failure didn't matter, what would I still do?

You don't need a perfect answer. Purpose often reveals itself in pieces and gets refined through experience.

Your purpose doesn't have to be loud. It just has to be real.

How Purpose Helps You Bend, Not Break

Let's return to the idea of the tree in the wind.

A tree bends and sways – but it doesn't float away. Why? Because it's rooted. Deeply.

Purpose is your root system. When external conditions shift, purpose holds you steady long enough to recalibrate, adapt, and rise again.

When you understand why you think and act the way you do, you will discover the ability to make changes that align what you do with who you want to be.

Practical Ways to Anchor in Purpose

☑ CREATE A "WHY" STATEMENT Write a short sentence that captures the impact you want to have. *Example: "I help people heal through storytelling." "I bring calm to chaotic environments." "I turn pain into beauty."*

☑ REVISIT YOUR WHY WEEKLY Set a reminder to read your purpose statement once a week. Let it reorient you.

☑ USE PURPOSE TO PRIORITIZE Ask: "Does this decision bring me closer to or further from my purpose?"

☑ RETURN TO IT IN THE CHAOS When everything feels uncertain, don't chase clarity - chase connection. Reconnect with your why, even when nothing else makes sense.

✿ Case Study: Jamal's Shift

Jamal was a product designer. Smart. Creative. Successful. But after layoffs hit, he spiralled. He'd tied his entire worth to his output. Without a job, he felt completely lost.

Through coaching, he discovered something crucial: what he loved most wasn't designing *products* - it was designing *experiences*. He wanted to help people feel empowered, clear, and cared for.

He took that purpose and started volunteering in education. Eventually, he launched a consulting practice in product design for public services, combining his skills with his newly rediscovered purpose.

The job changed. His identity shifted. But his purpose held steady.

● ● ●

❋ Final Reflection: Let Purpose Lead

You can change direction. You can slow down. You can pause. But when you're clear on your purpose, you never truly lose your way.

So, in times of uncertainty, remember this:

You don't need to know every step. You just need to know the direction you want to take.

Let your purpose be the constant in your ever-changing world.

Let it guide you when the wind picks up.

Let it remind you who you are when everything else shifts around you.

Let it root you – so you can bend without breaking.

❋ ❋ ❋

8

Emotional Agility

Surfing emotions instead of getting swept away

"Between stimulus and response, there is a space. In that space is our power to choose our response."

— Viktor E. Frankl

In life, you'll face setbacks, rejections, unexpected news, and personal failures. It's not a matter of if – it's when.

We often have no control over the events that we face, but we have absolute control over how we respond to them.

The question, therefore, isn't "Will I face a setback in my life?" but "How will I respond when I do?"

The answer lies in **emotional agility**.

For most of us, our emotions are fairly rigid. We are creatures of habit and tend to respond in the same way to the same event, time after time. If someone pushes us in a crowd today, we will react the same way as we did when someone pushed us in a crowd last week.

However, we don't have to respond the same way every time.

Instead of reacting immediately, we can pause, for a second, or even a fraction of a second, to consider the potential responses we have at our disposal.

This is emotional agility. The flexibility to choose how we will react. It gives you the ability to feel what you feel without being *ruled* by those feelings. It lets you acknowledge your emotions, learn from them, and respond thoughtfully rather than impulsively.

Emotional agility is your internal version of *bending with the breeze.*

What Is Emotional Agility?

Coined by psychologist Dr. Susan David, emotional agility is the ability to be with your emotions – both pleasant and unpleasant – in a way that's compassionate, curious, and courageous.

It means:

☑ You don't suppress your feelings.

☑ You don't let them control you.

☑ You recognize them as data – not directions.

You feel it. You name it. You stay open to it. You choose your response.

That's the power of emotional agility.

The Cost of Emotional Rigidity

We've all experienced emotional rigidity – when we:

☒ Get stuck thinking "I shouldn't feel this way."

☒ Avoid discomfort through distraction or overwork.

☒ React from anger or fear without pausing to reflect.

☒ Define ourselves by temporary feelings ("I'm just a failure.")

Rigid emotions become stuck emotions. And stuck emotions often create:

- ⊗ Conflict

- ⊗ Burnout

- ⊗ Impulsive decisions

- ⊗ Regret

- ⊗ Shame

Agility, on the other hand, creates flow. It opens you up and keeps your emotional life *in motion*.

The 4 Steps to Emotional Agility

1. Show Up to What You Feel

Don't suppress or sugarcoat. Be honest about what's happening inside.

Say:

- ✓ "I'm feeling anxious right now."

- ✓ "I notice tension in my chest."

- ✓ "I'm overwhelmed and uncertain."

Suppressing emotions doesn't make them disappear – it makes them louder later.

2. Step Out of the Emotion

Remember: you are not your feelings.

⊗ Avoid saying "I *am* angry."

✓ Try saying "I *notice* anger rising."

This subtle shift creates distance, a healthy pause between you and the emotion.

Mindfulness, breathwork, or simply naming your feeling out loud can help create this space.

3. Get Curious, Not Critical

Instead of harsh judgment ("Why am I like this?"), try gentle curiosity:

✓ "What's this emotion telling me?"

✓ "Where is this coming from?"

✓ "What do I need right now?"

Emotions are messengers, not enemies. Listen to what they're saying before you act.

4. Make a Values-Based Move

Now that you've paused, ask yourself:

✓ "What action aligns with the kind of person I want to be?"

That might mean speaking calmly instead of lashing out. Pausing instead of quitting. Offering grace instead of retreating.

You don't need to feel perfect to act with purpose. You just need to choose wisely - even when emotions run high.

Common Emotional Traps – And How to Escape

TRAP	EMOTIONALLY AGILE SHIFT
"I shouldn't feel this."	"It's okay to feel this. What's it telling me?"
"This always happens to me."	"This *happened*. But I have a choice now."
"I'll just avoid it."	"I can handle discomfort - and grow from it."
"I need to react right now."	"I'll take a breath and respond with care."

Case Study: Alana's Reframe

Alana had just been passed over for a promotion she thought she'd earned. Her first emotion was rage.

Her natural reaction was to express that rage by resigning and finding a new company which would appreciate what she had to offer. This had happened to her before, and this is how she reacted then. It caused a temporary delay in her career, but after a few months, she got back onto her feet and started again.

She called a friend to vent and vocalise her plans, but the friend managed to calm her and convince her to reflect before acting.

That evening, she reflected on the emotions she had felt. She instantly recognised that her anger was a result of the disappointment she felt at not getting the promotion which she believed was deserved. As she reflected further, she realised that this was accompanied by embarrassment.

She realised it wasn't just about the job. It was about her vision of herself and how she thought others would perceive her. She also remembered that the same thing had happened at her last job. Resigning hadn't moved her forward; it had just caused her to repeat history.

The following morning, she had a candid conversation with her manager, got honest feedback, and enrolled in a leadership course. A year later, she was awarded the promotion she wanted and her career blossomed.

❋ ❋ ❋

Practices to Build Emotional Agility

✅ THE NAME-IT PRACTICE At least once a day, name the strongest emotion you felt. Say: "I felt _____ when _____ happened." Naming creates clarity.

✅ THE BODY SCAN PAUSE Sit quietly for two minutes. Where do you feel tension? Emotion often shows up in the body first. Release it gently.

✅ THE COMPASSION QUESTION Ask: "If my best friend were feeling this, what would I say to them?" Then say it to yourself.

✅ THE VALUES JOURNAL At the end of each day, write down one small action you took that reflected who you want to be – even if you felt emotionally off-track.

Final Reflection: Feel It, Don't Fuel It

Emotional agility isn't about "fixing" your emotions. It's about relating to them differently.

You don't need to numb or dramatize what you feel. You just need to let it flow – *through* you, not *over* you. When your feelings have room to breathe, so do you.

And that's when your strongest, wisest self can finally speak.

Be strong like a tree, strong in its core, but soft like its leaves. Feel deeply. Bend gently. Move wisely.

9

Strategic Stillness

Why stepping back can be
your most powerful move

*"Sometimes, the most urgent and vital thing you
can possibly do is take a complete rest."*

ASHLEIGH BRILLIANT

In a culture obsessed with productivity, hustle, and momentum, the idea of pausing can feel like failure.

We're told:

"Keep going."

"Don't stop."

"Push through it."

But what if that relentless forward motion isn't strength - it's avoidance?

What if the wisest move isn't another push forward... but a strategic pause?

Strategic Stillness is about learning when to stop - not out of fear, but from wisdom. It's about **stillness**, not stagnation.

Stillness Is Not Just Doing Nothing

Stillness is not laziness, procrastination, or avoidance. It is the conscious choice to relax and be idle without any specific purpose or goal.

The Dutch have a word for it - "Niksen". The art of actively doing nothing. It is about giving yourself permission to simply be, allowing your mind to wander and recharge, and is a useful antidote to the constant pressures of daily life and the fight against physical, emotional and mental burnout.

Strategic stillness is a short-term, focused approach to stillness.

It is the conscious choice to pause before you act. It's the difference between reacting and responding. It is the physical manifestation of emotional agility, for example:

✅ Taking a breath before replying to a heated email.

✅ Spending a day walking in nature instead of pushing through burnout.

✅ Taking a week to reflect before jumping into the next project.

✅ Sitting with discomfort instead of rushing to fix it.

Stillness is not the enemy of progress - it's the environment where wisdom is born.

Why Stillness Feels So Uncomfortable

Stillness brings you face to face with yourself. Without the noise of busyness, your fears, doubts, and unresolved emotions rise to the surface.

And that's exactly where the growth happens.

When you pause long enough to *hear yourself think,* you create space for clarity to emerge.

But because we fear that discomfort, we often keep moving - chasing distractions, productivity, and dopamine hits instead of turning inward.

Stillness breaks that cycle.

When to Pause Instead of Push

Here are moments when stillness beats action:

WHEN YOU...	STILLNESS CAN...
Feel confused or overwhelmed	Create clarity
Feel emotionally reactive	Allow grounding
Are in transition	Invite alignment
Have multiple paths forward	Support decision-making
Sense burnout	Enable recovery

Movement without direction is chaos. Stillness brings the map.

The Benefits of Strategic Stillness

☑ MENTAL CLARITY: When you stop doing, you start noticing.

☑ EMOTIONAL REGULATION: Emotions process better when you don't ignore or rush them.

☑ CREATIVE INSIGHT: Ideas often emerge in quiet spaces, not during the noise of execution.

☑ ALIGNED ACTION: You stop reacting impulsively and start acting intentionally

Case Study: Daniel's Reset

Daniel was a high performer, a marketing director, father of two, a marathon runner. On paper, he was crushing life. Internally, he was unravelling.

He sought out coaching, expecting to discover ways to become even more productive. Instead, he got a two-word assignment:

"Stop everything."

For 48 hours, Daniel did nothing "productive." No work. No problem-solving. Just walking, journaling, and being present.

What surfaced surprised him. He realised he didn't want to climb higher at work; he wanted out entirely. He wanted to create, to write, to teach.

That insight didn't come from movement. It came from stillness.

❀ ❀ ❀

Practicing Strategic Stillness

You don't need a week-long retreat. You need a few intentional moments.

1. The Pause Practice

Before responding to anything stressful, take one deep breath. Ask: "Is this reaction aligned with who I want to be?"

2. The Weekly Reset

Choose a time each week (even 30 minutes) to do nothing. No phone. No talking. No consuming. Just listen. Walk. Breathe. What comes up?

3. The Reflection Ritual

Each evening or weekend, ask:

- ☑ What felt good this week?
- ☑ What drained me?
- ☑ What do I need more of – or less of?

Write it down. Let your truth emerge from the quiet.

4. Wait Before You Decide

Before making any major decision, sleep on it. Give stillness space to speak. If it feels right today, it will still feel right tomorrow.

Stillness as a Strength

You've been taught to hustle. You've been praised for staying productive. But here's a radical truth:

Sometimes, your power lives in your pause.

When you stop long enough to listen inward, your next move becomes clearer, stronger, and more authentic. Stillness doesn't delay your path – it *clarifies* it.

Final Reflection: In Stillness, You Realign

The world will push you to move faster. But your soul may be asking for silence.

Honour that call.

Stillness is how you bend without breaking. It's how you hear what your body, heart, and spirit have been trying to tell you. And it's how you prepare for your next right move. So, when in doubt, stop. Breathe. Wait. Listen.

The breeze may be shifting. Stillness will help you feel which way it is blowing.

10

The Secret of Life – Enjoying the Passage of Time

Focusing on the journey
rather than just the
destination

"The secret o' life is enjoying the passage of time"
JAMES TAYLOR

What if joy isn't found in crossing the finish line, but in *walking the path itself?*

What if success isn't measured by how fast you move, but by how present you remain along the way?

In a world that worships speed, ambition, and achievement, this idea might feel radical, but it's one of the most liberating truths you'll ever discover:

Time isn't just something to manage. It's something to savour.

You weren't meant to race through your life; you were meant to live it.

What "Enjoying the Passage of Time" Really Means

It doesn't mean pretending everything is perfect.

It doesn't mean ignoring pain or forcing a smile during struggle.

It means learning to *be with* time, not chase it.

It means choosing to *notice* the small moments - the breath, the laugh, the sunlight - rather than constantly sprinting toward the next milestone.

Why We Rush Through Life

From childhood, we're taught that happiness lives in the future:

☑ "When I get that job..."

☑ "When I meet the right person..."

☑ "When I'm finally financially secure..."

But the future is a moving target. By the time we reach it, our expectations have already shifted. So, we live in a constant loop of delay:

Work now. Enjoy later.
Suffer now. Succeed later.

But what if later never comes?

What if joy isn't a reward for effort, but a companion to it?

The Problem with Always Looking Ahead

Planning is wise. Preparing is smart.

But living exclusively in "what's next" makes you miss what's *now*.

☑ You drink coffee while planning your next meeting – missing the warmth in your hands.

☑ You go for a walk while thinking about all the unread messages in your inbox – missing the breeze on your face.

☑ You cross the finish line of a goal – then forget to celebrate before rushing to the next race.

This isn't life. This is motion sickness.

The antidote is presence.

The Power of Present-Minded Living

When you stop chasing time, time opens up.

When you start enjoying the passage of time:

☑ ORDINARY MOMENTS BECOME SACRED. A morning cup of tea transforms from routine into ritual.

☑ YOU STOP POSTPONING HAPPINESS. Joy becomes available now, not someday.

☑ YOU CREATE EMOTIONAL STABILITY. Anxiety fades when your mind returns from the future and focuses on the present.

You begin to *feel your life*, not just survive it.

Case Study: Evan's Shift

Evan had a full calendar and an empty heart.

He was always busy, always producing, always chasing "enough." Until, one day, sitting in a quiet café, he watched an older couple share a dessert without a word but with smiles on their faces.

There was a calmness and serenity about them.

He realised: *They're not rushing. They're just here, enjoying the moment.*

It hit him harder than any productivity seminar ever had.

Evan didn't quit his job or move to a farm. He simply began showing up - to his meals, his walks, his friendships - with more intention and less urgency.

Life started to feel *full*, even when it was simple.

❋ ❋ ❋

Practices for Savouring Time

1. Ritualise One Ordinary Moment Each Day

Choose something mundane - your shower, coffee, walk - and turn it into a ritual. Slow it down. Feel it. Be in it fully.

2. Create "Slow Time"

Set aside 30-60 minutes each week for absolutely nothing. No multitasking. Just existing. Let time flow without trying to capture or "use" it.

3. Single-Task with Intention

Practice doing one thing at a time. No background music, no scrolling, no rushing. Just one complete experience.

4. Capture Beauty, Not Just Tasks

Rather than photographing everything for social media, take mental snapshots of genuine beauty: a friend's smile, sunlight through leaves, a moment of shared silence.

Joy as a Metric of Success

What if you measured your life not by your accomplishments, but by how much you truly enjoyed?

Try asking yourself:

☑ Did I feel something real today?

☑ Did I pause long enough to notice beauty around me?

☑ Did I give myself permission to enjoy this moment, even if it wasn't "productive"?

Because at the end of your life, you won't remember your to-do lists. You'll remember how you felt – the laughter, the stillness, the love.

Final Reflection: Don't Just Pass Through Time – Let It Pass Through You

Time isn't an enemy or a threat. It's a companion, a canvas, a river.

You don't need to rush to keep up with it.

You can walk alongside it. Rest with it. Laugh with it.

So slow down. Breathe deeply. Feel the breeze. Watch the sky shift. Be present.

Because the secret of life?

It was never about reaching the destination. It was about savouring the journey.

11

Creative Rerouting

Developing new solutions
under pressure with calm
clarity

*"Obstacles are those frightful things you see
when you take your eyes off your goal."*
<small>HENRY FORD</small>

What do you do when the path ahead gets blocked?

Do you wait? Give up? Double down and push harder?

Or do you find another way?

Life's challenges rarely come with warning signs or GPS alternatives. Yet the people who thrive - those who bend without breaking - aren't the ones with all the answers. They're the ones who master the art of improvisation.

When life slams a door shut, most of us stand there staring, disappointed, frustrated, bewildered.

But what if, instead of trying to force that same door open, you simply walked around it? Or climbed through a window? Or built your own door entirely?

This is the art of **creative rerouting** - the ability to find innovative, unexpected paths when your original route hits a wall.

From Problem-Focus to Possibility-Focus

When something goes wrong, most people slip into fix-it mode. They zoom in on what's broken, what's lost, what's unfair.

But zooming out often reveals better answers than zooming in.

Instead of obsessing over the blocked road, look around. Ask yourself:

☑ "What else could work?"

☑️ "What haven't I tried yet?"

☑️ "What am I assuming is solid that might actually be flexible?"

Creative rerouting starts not with more information, but with better questions.

Creative rerouting is the ability to reimagine how you'll reach a goal, without abandoning the goal itself.

It means:

☑️ Taking a detour without losing direction.

☑️ Shifting form while staying true to purpose.

☑️ Adapting with innovation, not resignation.

It's what musicians do when they improvise. What entrepreneurs do when a product flops. What you do when life hands you something you didn't plan for.

It's survival through imagination.

Obstacles as Invitations

A blocked path doesn't signal failure - it offers feedback.

Ask yourself:

☑️ "What is this challenge trying to teach me?"

☑️ "How could I approach this from a completely new angle?"

☑ "What would I try if I wasn't afraid of failing?"

Every limitation sparks creativity.

Some of the greatest inventions, art, and discoveries emerged from constraint, not comfort.

The Brain Loves Patterns (Even When They Stop Working)

Your brain is wired to repeat what feels familiar. This keeps you efficient, but it also keeps you stuck.

When your go-to strategy stops working, your first instinct might be to try it *again*, only harder.

But that's not resilience. That's rigidity.

True adaptability means being willing to let go of what once worked and experiment with something new.

Rerouting requires imagination. Imagination is a muscle. You can train it.

Framework: The 3Rs of Creative Rerouting

1. Recognize
Name the block. What exactly isn't working? Get specific.

⊗ *"I'm not getting callbacks from job applications"*

⊗ *"My workouts no longer energize me"*

⊗ *"I'm losing interest in this project"*

2. Reimagine

Brainstorm at least three alternatives, no matter how unconventional they seem.

☑ CHANGE THE METHOD: *What if you tried a completely different approach?*

☑ CHANGE THE GOAL: *Could you redefine what "success" actually looks like?*

☑ CHANGE THE TIMELINE: What if this took longer, and that was perfectly okay?

3. Re-engage

Test your best option. Not permanently. Just as an experiment. Then gather feedback and adjust accordingly.

Adaptation isn't a one-time decision. It's a continual recalibration.

Case Study: Tara's Pivot

Tara was a wedding photographer whose business collapsed during a global shutdown.

At first, she panicked. Then, she got curious.

She realised she didn't just love photography, she loved *telling love stories* and to date, she had told these stories through her photographs.

So, she started offering online storytelling sessions for couples and families and began writing people's relationship stories as keepsake books.

Her business returned differently, creatively, and more aligned than ever.

The plan changed. The purpose didn't. That's creative rerouting in action.

● ● ●

Exercises to Build Your Rerouting Reflex

☑ OBSTACLE MAP List three current roadblocks. For each, brainstorm three "weird" alternatives - even if they sound silly. Allow absurdity. Creativity follows permission.

☑ REVERSE THE ASSUMPTION Take one stuck problem and flip the core assumption. Instead of "I need more time," ask "What if I had *less* time?" What new solutions emerge?

☑ INSPIRATION SWIPE Look at how nature, children, or other industries solve problems. Ask: "How would a child/artist/engineer/academic tackle this?"

Final Reflection: Reinvention Is a Skill

You don't need to be fearless to be creative.

You just need to be willing to try again - differently.

Because every roadblock isn't the end of the road. It's a nudge.

Look around. Try again. Reroute. Rise.

12

Micro-Moves, Macro Wins

The power of small,
intentional actions

"Small deeds done are better than
great deeds planned."

PETER MARSHALL

Inspiration is loud. Change is often quiet.

We love big breakthroughs, dramatic transformations, and all-or-nothing declarations. But real growth usually happens in quieter ways – through **micro-moves.**

Micro-moves are small, intentional actions that compound over time. They're flexible, doable, and sustainable. They don't rely on motivation – they create momentum.

Micro-moves help you to use **tiny shifts** to create **massive impact.**

Why We Wait for "Big"

We tell ourselves:

⊗ "If I can't go to the gym for an hour, it's not worth it."

⊗ "If I can't write a chapter, I won't write a word."

⊗ "If I'm not ready to launch, I won't start at all."

But this perfectionism disguised as productivity is really procrastination in disguise.

What you need isn't a heroic leap. You need a small, repeatable movement forward.

Tiny steps beat stalled intentions every time.

The Compound Effect in Real Life

Small efforts, done consistently, lead to major results:

☑ 10 minutes of journaling builds self-awareness.

☑ 1 intentional conversation per week transforms a
relationship.

☑ 5 push-ups a day sparks a wellness habit.

☑ 1 "no" a week reclaims your time.

The magic isn't in the scale. It's in the **consistency**.

The Micro-Move Method

1. Shrink the Step

Take your goal and reduce it to the smallest possible action.

☑ Want to meditate daily? Start with 1 minute.

☑ Want to write a book? Start with 1 paragraph.

☑ Want to build confidence? Start with 1 brave moment a day.

2. Make It Repeatable

Tie your micro-move to a specific time, trigger, or existing habit.

Examples:

✅ "After I brush my teeth, I'll do one breathing exercise."

✅ "On Mondays, I'll plan one joyful event for the week."

✅ "Every morning, I'll ask: What's one thing I can complete today?"

3. Track and Celebrate

Keep a visible log. Celebrate consistency over intensity.

Progress builds identity. Identity builds momentum. Momentum builds change.

Case Study: Omar's Tiny Habit

Omar wanted to start his own business, but the thought overwhelmed him completely.

Instead of quitting his job, he committed to just 15 minutes each night to sketch ideas. That 15 minutes turned into 30. Then a business plan. Then a client. Then a full-time leap, two years later.

What started as a micro-move created a macro impact.

● ● ●

Micro-Moves for Key Areas of Life

GOAL	MICRO-MOVE EXAMPLE
Build confidence	Speak up once per meeting
Improve health	Drink 1 more glass of water each day
Strengthen relationships	Send one check-in text per week
Manage stress	Breathe deeply before opening your inbox
Spark creativity	Doodle or free-write for 3 minutes a day

Final Reflection: Don't Wait to Move Mountains – Move Pebbles

We often delay change because we think it must be dramatic. We imagine transformation as a grand event, a complete career pivot, a 30-day cleanse, a bold leap. But the most sustainable changes rarely start with a bang.

They start with a breath.

They start with one tiny action taken with care and intention.

Micro-moves are the quiet revolution of personal growth. They whisper what perfectionism drowns out: "Start small. Start messy. But start."

Every time you take a micro-move, you cast a vote for who you're becoming. You declare: "Even now, even with doubt, fatigue, or fear, I'm still choosing to move forward."

And when you stack enough of those votes, you become that version of yourself. Not through a dramatic reinvention, but through a gentle unfolding.

So, if today feels heavy, ask yourself:

☑ What's one thing I can do for two minutes?

☑ What's one pebble I can move to shift the path?

☑ What would progress look like if it didn't need to be perfect?

This is how the overwhelmed become focused.

This is how the stuck get unstuck.

This is how you move mountains, one deliberate pebble at a time.

Don't wait for ideal conditions. Don't wait for clarity or confidence.

Just move one pebble. Then another.

And trust that one day, you'll look back and realise:

The shift wasn't sudden.

But it was seismic.

13

Building Your Personal Ecosystem

Designing a life that
supports flexibility

"You do not rise to the level of your goals.
You fall to the level of your systems."
JAMES CLEAR

You've learned how to bend instead of break. You've practised purpose, stillness, emotional agility, and micro-moves.

But here's the truth that will make or break your long-term growth:

Your habits are only as strong as the environment that surrounds them.

Just as a plant needs the right soil, light, and water to thrive, you need the right ecosystem. An intentional mix of people, practices, and spaces to sustain your growth.

Building your own Personal Ecosystem will enable you to design a life that helps you flex without friction.

What Is a Personal Ecosystem?

Your personal ecosystem is everything around you that shapes your mindset, motivation, and energy.

It includes:

- ✅ RELATIONSHIPS – Who lifts you up or drains you?

- ✅ ROUTINES – What rhythms energize or exhaust you?

- ✅ ENVIRONMENTS – Where do you feel most alive or most depleted?

- ✅ INFORMATION DIET – What are you feeding your mind each day?

If you want to stay resilient and adaptive, your life must support that resilience, not sabotage it.

Why Environments Beat Willpower Every Time

Willpower is useful – but it runs out.

You can try to force focus in a chaotic space, or you can create a space that naturally fosters focus. You can try to resist negativity all day, or spend more time with people who naturally lift you up.

The best way to sustain change is to make it easier to do the right thing and harder to do the wrong thing.

That's the power of ecosystems.

1. People: Curate Your Circle

Who's in your greenhouse?

Relationships either grow you or stunt you. Pay attention to:

☑ Who you feel ENERGIZED around.

☒ Who leaves you DRAINED, DOUBTFUL, or DEFENSIVE.

☑ Who reflects back your VALUES, not just your past.

Questions to ask yourself:

☑ Who in my life helps me think more creatively?

☑ Who encourages my flexibility and growth?

☑ Who do I feel safe being real around?

Action:

Make a list of your five closest people. Next to each name, write how they affect your mindset on a weekly basis. Then, *nurture the nourishing, limit the draining.*

2. Routines: Design Rhythms, Not Rigidity

Your days don't need tight scheduling, but they should have rhythms that ground you.

A flexible life still needs structure - just the kind that adapts with you.

Examples:

- ✅ A MONDAY MORNING RITUAL to align your week with your purpose.

- ✅ A MIDDAY RESET (walk, breathwork, unplug) to regroup.

- ✅ A FRIDAY REVIEW to reflect on what worked and what to release.

Ask:

- ✅ What rituals support my emotional agility?

- ✅ What small daily or weekly rhythms help me stay aligned?

Then embed those patterns gently into your calendar. Not as obligations - but as supports.

3. Environments: Set the Stage for Growth

Just as some plants thrive in sunlight while others prefer shade, your environment matters deeply.

Audit your spaces:

☑ What does your workspace feel like?

☑ Is your home cluttered or calming?

☑ Where do you go when you need to recharge?

Tiny upgrades make a big difference:

☑ Add a calming object or candle to your desk.

☑ Designate a "tech-free zone" in your home.

☑ Rearrange your physical space for less friction and more flow.

Your outer space reflects – and shapes – your inner state.

4. Inputs: Curate What Comes In

You constantly absorb input: conversations, news, podcasts, emails, and endless scrolling. Most of it isn't neutral – it either feeds your fears, numbs you out, or energises you.

Be deliberate.

Ask yourself:

☑ Does this feed my fear or fuel my purpose?

☑ Am I learning something helpful, or just distracting myself?

Create boundaries:

- ☑ Silence or unfollow accounts that drain your energy.

- ☑ Replace mindless consumption with mindful content.

- ☑ Schedule intentional consumption (like 20 minutes of inspiring reading instead of 2 hours of doom-scrolling through social feeds).

Your attention is a garden. What are you choosing to plant?

Case Study: Layla's Life Rebuild

After a brutal year of burnout, Layla realised she didn't need another productivity hack, she needed an ecosystem shift.

Here's what she did:

- ☑ Released two draining friendships that no longer served her.

- ☑ Created a Sunday evening "quiet hour" with tea and journaling.

- ☑ Transformed her cluttered office into a simple, plant-filled sanctuary.

- ☑ Swapped her morning social media scroll for a 5-minute affirmation playlist.

She didn't change jobs or move cities. But her life began to feel wildly different – more rooted, more resilient, more *hers*.

The shifts were small, but they supported her inner transformation like rich soil nurtures a seed.

※ ※ ※

Final Reflection: Design for Who You're Becoming

You're not just building habits. You're becoming someone new.

Ask yourself:

- ✓ Does my environment reflect who I want to be?

- ✓ Do my relationships support how I want to live?

- ✓ Does my daily life create space for joy, flexibility, and rest?

You don't need a perfect life. You need a supportive one.

The breeze will keep blowing. You can't control that. But you can build a garden that thrives in the wind.

≈ ≈ ≈

14

Integration, Not Inspiration

Making it real, making it yours

"Knowledge is only a rumour until it lives in the muscle."

You've read. You've reflected. You've absorbed new ideas.

Now what?

The greatest risk at this stage isn't failure. It's *inspiration without integration.*

Here's the truth: you don't need more "aha!" moments.

You need to *live differently.*

Integration marks your turning point from understanding *in theory* to applying *in practice.* From admiring change to *embodying* it.

Why Insight Alone Isn't Enough

We love the dopamine hit of inspiration:

☑ A powerful quote that stops us in our tracks.

☑ A lightbulb moment during a podcast.

☑ A fresh perspective that shifts everything.

But inspiration without follow-through becomes a pointless loop:

Get Inspired

Feel Good

Do Nothing

Wonder Why Nothing's Changed

Inspiration is the spark. *Integration* is the fire.

It's not what you know – it's what you do *with what you know.*

The Integration Gap: Where Most People Stop

Here's the predictable pattern after someone finishes a personal growth book or course:

☑ They feel genuinely moved.

☑ They underline and highlight key passages.

☑ They excitedly tell a friend about their discoveries.

☒ They change... *absolutely nothing.*

Not because they don't care. But because they lack a **system for living the lesson**.

Integration helps you build that system.

Integration ≠ Overhaul.
Integration = Embedding.

You don't need to flip your life upside down. You need to **weave change into your real, messy, ordinary life.**

Integration means:

☑ Adapting tools to fit *your* actual context.

☑ Turning abstract ideas into concrete habits.

☑ Designing small rituals that keep you aligned with who you want to become.

Step 1: Choose One Practice to Live This Week

From everything you've absorbed so far, pick **one concept** that hit you in the gut.

Maybe it's:

- ☑ Pausing three seconds before reacting.

- ☑ Reframing that recent failure as an opportunity to learn.

- ☑ Taking one micro-step toward your biggest goal.

- ☑ Creating a five-minute morning ritual that grounds you.

Now make it daily. Tie it to something you already do (like writing one intention every time you drink your morning coffee).

Don't wait for the perfect moment. Start *small* and start *now*.

Step 2: Create a Reminder System

New ways of thinking need **reminders**, not superhuman willpower.

Try:

- ☑ A sticky note on your bathroom mirror ("Bend, don't break.")

- ☑ A phone lock screen featuring your purpose statement.

- ☑ A weekly calendar reminder: "Am I moving how I want to live?"

Make the invisible visible.

Step 3: Reflect, Refine, Repeat

At the end of each week, pause and ask:

✓ What's actually working?

✓ What's falling flat?

✓ What tiny adjustment can I make next week?

Integration is iterative. Don't chase perfection - chase progress that *feels like you*.

Designing Your "Bend with the Breeze" Rituals

Here are a few integration rituals you can adopt:

RITUAL NAME	WHAT IT DOES	HOW TO DO IT
SUNDAY RESET	Reconnects you to purpose and alignment	Journal for 15 minutes: What matters this week? Where can I flex?
MORNING CENTRING	Sets emotional tone for the day	3 deep breaths + read your "North Star" statement
EVENING DEBRIEF	Tracks emotional agility and learning	Ask: Did I bend today? What did I learn? What felt heavy?
WEEKLY DETOUR CHECK	Builds a resilience mindset	Reflect on unexpected changes - what did they teach you?

You don't need to do them all. Start with **one**. Make it yours. Adjust as needed.

Case Study: Priya's Integration Process

Priya used to consume self-help content voraciously but struggled to implement any of it.

After reading the earlier chapters of this book, she chose to focus on just one shift: "Pause before responding."

She tied it to email – every time she received a tense message, she waited 10 minutes before replying.

She set a weekly calendar reminder: *"How did I respond to stress this week?"*

Three weeks in, she noticed something profound:

☑ Fewer arguments.

☑ Less regret.

☑ A growing sense of internal calm.

The change wasn't flashy. But it was *real*. And it was *hers*.

● ● ●

What You Repeat, You Become

There's a version of you – calmer, more agile, more present – already forming.

But that version doesn't arrive through inspiration alone. It arrives through **repetition**.

- ✅ Repetition of intention.

- ✅ Repetition of awareness.

- ✅ Repetition of small, aligned actions.

You don't need to "become a new person." You just need to return to the truest version of yourself, over and over again.

🌬️ Final Reflection: Embody, Don't Just Understand

You have more than enough insight. Now is the time to *move differently. To pause more often. To reframe setbacks faster. To trust flexibility as your superpower.*

So don't leave this book feeling inspired. Leave it *transformed.*

And transformation doesn't live in your head.

It lives in your hands. In your breath. In the day-to-day way you show up.

Make it yours. Make it real.

Make it live in your muscle.

🌬️ 🌬️ 🌬️

15

The Flower and the Storm

Reclaiming softness as
strength, finding mastery
through movement

*"The oak fought the wind and was broken; the
willow bent when it must and survived."*

Robert Jordan

When you think of strength, what image comes to mind?

A mountain? A soldier? A tower?

Now imagine something different: A delicate flower, rooted deep in soil, reaching toward the sun. A stem that bends without snapping. Petals that reopen after the rain passes.

This isn't weakness. This is strength of the highest kind.

The strength to be *present*, not perfect. The strength to *flex* when life doesn't go your way. The strength to *return to the light*, even after bending in the storm.

This is the flower. This is you.

Why We Mistake Rigidity for Strength

We've been sold a story that to be strong means:

☑ Holding your ground at all costs.

☑ Hiding your emotions.

☑ Charging forward without hesitation.

But that kind of strength often creates:

☒ Burnout.

☒ Isolation.

☒ Collapse when conditions shift.

True strength isn't about standing firm. It's about knowing **when and how to yield** - *without* losing your foundation.

The Flower's Power

Let's revisit the flower, your final metaphor:

☑ It reaches for the light - DIRECTION.

☑ It roots deep in the soil - STABILITY.

☑ It bends with the breeze - ADAPTABILITY.

☑ It blossoms fully - EXPRESSION.

☑ It closes and opens again - RESILIENCE.

Your journey, like the flower's, isn't linear. It's seasonal. Rhythmic. Alive.

The storm will come. It always does.

But if you're rooted in purpose... If you've built emotional agility... If you've practised bending instead of breaking, then you will sway. You will adapt. And when the wind passes, you will rise - more open, more grounded, more *you*.

Being Present in the Storm

Sometimes you can't see the sun. You're in survival mode. The wind is loud.

In these moments, strength looks like:

- ☑ Taking one deep breath.
- ☑ Saying no with grace.
- ☑ Resting instead of pushing.
- ☑ Asking for help.
- ☑ Noticing beauty, even in the dark.

Presence isn't passive. It's a powerful response to chaos.

To be present in the storm is to choose peace over panic. To bend without losing yourself.

🌼 Case Study: Jonah's Return

Jonah was always "the strong one." A leader, a problem-solver, a doer.

Then his marriage ended. His job followed. For the first time, pushing through stopped working. At first, he felt lost. Weak.

But something shifted when he stopped fighting the storm and started listening to it. He took long walks. Journaled. Reconnected with old friends. Cried - something he hadn't allowed himself to do in years.

He began to see that his softness didn't make him less strong - it made him *human*. Eventually, Jonah built a new life. Slower.

Truer. More rooted in who he really was, not who he felt he had to be.

● ● ●

Your Life, Like the Flower's

This book began with a challenge: Don't just push through. Learn to bend. Now it ends with a blessing:

Be like a flower - strong enough to turn your face to the sun, flexible enough to bend with the breeze, and rooted enough to rise again after every storm.

You don't have to live a hard life to live a strong one. You don't have to break to prove your strength. You don't have to control the weather to keep growing.

Your softness isn't a liability. It's your wisdom. Your artistry. Your power.

Final Reflection – Flexibility over Rigidity

Ask yourself:

☑ Where in my life am I still trying to force instead of flow?

☑ What part of me needs less pressure and more presence?

☑ How can I honour my own season today?

Let go of the myth that strength means never falling. Fall. Bend. Pause. Rise again. *Because the strongest things in nature don't resist the wind. They dance with it. And they survive.*

Conclusion

Becoming at One with the Breeze

A final invitation to choose
flow over force and create
a life that moves with you,
not against you

*"You can't stop the waves,
but you can learn to surf."*
JON KABAT-ZINN

You made it. Through the metaphors, the mindset shifts, and the methods. You've explored how to bend without breaking, how to reroute without quitting, how to shift from force to flow.

And now, there's only one thing left to do: **become at one with the breeze.**

This doesn't mean becoming passive or directionless. It means becoming someone who moves *with* life, not against it.

Someone who adapts – not from fear, but from wisdom. Someone who responds – not with panic, but with presence. Someone who grows – not in straight lines, but in spirals and seasons.

This is what it means to *live* the concept of bending with the breeze.

What It Means to Become at One with the Breeze

You're no longer chasing a rigid version of success.

Now, you're guided by:

☑ PURPOSE, not pressure.

☑ ADAPTABILITY, not perfection.

☑ CLARITY, not control.

☑ STEADINESS, not speed.

You've built inner tools:

☑ Emotional agility.

- ✅ Strategic stillness.

- ✅ Creative rerouting.

- ✅ Integration rituals.

But tools only become powerful when you use them.

So, the final step isn't learning more. The final step is living it.

Start Where You Are

You don't need to overhaul your life overnight. You don't need a dramatic reinvention.

You only need to wake up each day and ask:

- ✅ Where can I soften?

- ✅ Where can I pause?

- ✅ Where can I move forward – differently?

Let that question shape your day. Let it reshape your life.

Give Yourself Permission

To not know. To go slow. To bloom late. To grow unevenly. To rest without guilt. To start over again and again.

Because mastery isn't found in being flawless. It's found in returning. Gently. Often.

You Are at One with the Breeze

This book gave you a framework. But you bring it to life.

So let your days reflect the truth you now know:

You can be focused and flexible. Resilient and soft. Purposeful and peaceful.

You are not the storm. You are not the broken branch. You are the flower that bends. You are the roots that hold. You are at one with the breeze itself.

Final Blessing

May you trust your own rhythm.

May you move with grace, not grinding effort.

May you grow through whatever you face.

May you bend and sway and rise again.

And when life shifts, because it always does, may you remember:

You are not here to resist the wind.

You are here to dance with it.

You are not just bending with the breeze.

You are at one with it.

Expanded Toolkit Worksheets

Worksheet 1: Cultivating Flexible Focus

INSTRUCTIONS: Commit to setting aside a few minutes at the start or end of your day (or week) to complete this worksheet. Reflect honestly on your experiences, note any adjustments you make, and celebrate the moments when you effectively "bend with the breeze." This tool helps you track your progress, pinpoint areas for growth, and reinforce your ability to adapt when life throws you curveballs.

Section 1: Daily Reflection and Mindfulness

✅ SET YOUR INTENTION:

- **Question:** What flexible focus intention do I want to carry into today?

- **Your Answer:** _____

  _____

  _____

✅ MINDFUL CHECK-IN:

- **Question**: How do I feel physically and emotionally right now?

- **Your Answer:** _____

  _____

  _____

✅ OBSERVATION OF FLEXIBILITY:

- **Question:** Describe one moment today when you consciously chose to be flexible or adapt your approach.

- **Your Answer:** _____

_____

_____

- **Impact:** _____

_____

_____

- **Question:** What positive result or insight emerged from that moment of flexibility?

- **Your Answer:** _____

_____

_____

Section 2: Adaptive Micro-Moves

☑ DEFINE A GOAL:

- **Question:** What is one overall goal you're working toward? (It can be personal, professional, or creative.)

- **Your Answer:** _____

☑ BREAK IT DOWN:

- **Task:** List at least three micro-moves (small actionable steps) that can help you progress toward this goal – steps you can adapt as needed.

- **Your Answer:** _____

☑ REFLECTION ON FLEXIBILITY:

- **Question:** Did you need to adjust any of these steps today? If so, what did you change and why?

- **Your Answer:** _____

Section 3: Obstacle Mapping & Redirection

☑ IDENTIFY A CHALLENGE:

- **Question:** Describe an obstacle or challenge you faced today.

- **Your Answer:** _____

_____

_____

☑ BRAINSTORM ALTERNATIVES:

- **Task:** List three different ways to tackle this obstacle.

- **Alternative 1:** _____

_____

_____

- **Alternative 2:** _____

_____

_____

- **Alternative 3:** _____

_____

_____

✓ REFLECT ON OUTCOME:

- **Question:** Which alternative did you try, and what was the outcome?

- **Your Answer:** _____

_____

_____

Section 4: Engagement with Nature & Movement
✓ NATURE CONNECTION:

- **Question:** Did you spend time in nature or engage in mindful physical movement today (such as walking, yoga, or dancing)? If so, describe the experience.

- **Your Answer:** _____

_____

_____

✓ IMPACT ON YOUR PERSPECTIVE:

- **Question:** How did this connection help you stay flexible or feel rejuvenated?

- **Your Answer:** _____

_____

_____

Section 5: Weekly Review Reflection (Complete weekly)

✓ SUMMARIZE YOUR LEARNING:

- **Question:** What's one significant lesson about flexible focus you discovered this week?

- **Your Answer:** _____

_____

_____

- **Assess Progress:**

- **Question:** Identify three positive changes in your mindset or actions that emerged from practicing flexibility.

- **Your Answer:** _____

_____

_____

✓ PLAN FOR THE FUTURE:

- **Question:** Which flexible practices will you maintain or adjust in the coming week?

- **Your Answer:** _____

_____

_____

✅ FINAL WEEKLY REFLECTION:

- **Question:** Write a brief reflection on how integrating flexible focus into your daily routine has affected your overall well-being and approach to challenges.

- **Your Answer:** _____

_____

_____

🍃 Final Reflections

Take a moment to capture your overall feelings about your journey toward flexible focus. How will you use these insights to shape your future decisions and growth?

🍃 🍃 🍃

- **Your summary:** _____

_____

_____

If you regularly engage with this worksheet, you'll build a habit of mindful reflection and adaptive planning. Over time, these small, intentional practices help you transform challenges into opportunities, conserve your energy, and cultivate a more resilient, joy-filled life. Remember: every instance of bending with the breeze is a moment of strength, not surrender.

Worksheet 2: The Purpose Clarifier

Objective: Reconnect with your deeper "why" so you can adapt your approach without losing sight of your vision.

What is my current goal?

Why is this goal important to me? (What emotional or practical need does it meet?)

What deeper values does this goal connect to?

☐ Growth   ☐ Contribution

☐ Security   ☐ Freedom

☐ Connection   ☐ Joy

☐ Other: _____

Can I achieve this purpose through another path if needed?

What might that look like?

My purpose statement:

I am committed to _____ *because it aligns with my values of* _____

I remain open to flexible ways of achieving it.

Worksheet 3: The Roadblock Re-framer

Objective: Reframe obstacles as detours, not dead ends.

Describe the current roadblock you're facing:

What emotions are you experiencing about this?

☐ Frustration   ☐ Disappointment

☐ Anxiety   ☐ Hopelessness

☐ Shame

☐ Other: _____

What is one helpful belief I can choose instead of dwelling on this emotion? *E.g., "This is teaching me patience" or "This isn't the only way."*

List two new possible responses or actions you could take:

Worksheet 4: The Flexibility Journal

Objective: Build awareness of your progress in shifting and adapting.

Date: _____

What challenge did I face today?

How did I respond at first?

How did I shift my approach or mindset?

What did I learn from bending instead of pushing harder?

What would I do again in the future?

Worksheet 5: The Emotional Agility Check-In

Objective: Practice emotional awareness and response flexibility.

1. How do I feel right now?

☐ Calm   ☐ Tense

☐ Sad   ☐ Excited

☐ Anxious   ☐ Grateful

☐ Other: _____

2. What triggered this emotion?

3. What is this emotion trying to tell me?

4. What do I need right now to support myself?

☐ A break   ☐ A walk

☐ To Journal   ☐ To talk to someone

☐ To change my thoughts

☐ Other: _____

5. What small action can I take to honour or release this emotion?

Your Personal Bending with the Breeze
30 Day Challenge

By incorporating these daily activities and challenges into your life over the next 30 days, you will equip yourself with all you need to integrate the principles of Bending with the Breeze into your life.

Week 1: Establishing the Mindset

Day 1: Embrace the Metaphor of Bending

Theme: Bending vs. Breaking (Introduction)

Activity:

Read the **Introduction,** focusing on the metaphor of how trees that bend survive storms while rigid ones break.

In your journal, answer: "Recall a time when I forced something and ended up drained - what might have happened if I bent instead?"

Prompt: See the passage describing willow trees as a model of adaptive living.

Day 2: Identify Drift

Theme: Recognizing Aimlessness (Chapter 1)

Activity:

Revisit the section **"The Quiet Trap of Drifting"**, noting the four common reasons people drift:

- ⊗ Fear of failure
- ⊗ Paralysis of too many choices
- ⊗ Comfort of avoidance
- ⊗ Myth of sudden clarity

List areas in your life where you sense drift (e.g., career, relationships, creativity).

Prompt: Use those four categories to pinpoint exactly why each area feels stuck.

Day 3: Take a Micro-Move Out of Drift

Theme: The Power of Tiny Steps (Chapter 1)

Activity:

Choose **one tiny action** (a "micro-move") toward any area you identified yesterday – for example:

- ⊗ Spend 10 minutes researching a course you've been curious about

☑ Send one introductory email to a potential mentor/coach

☑ Jot down a 3-item brainstorm list

Complete that micro-move today, no matter how small.

Prompt: Notice how even a ten-minute action builds momentum (see "Micro-Moves, Macro Wins")

Day 4: Reframe Goals as Joyful

Theme: Balancing Ambition and Well-being (Chapter 2)

Activity:

List your top three long-term goals. Next to each, write one way that obsessing over it could drain your joy.

For one goal, design a micro-move that feels intrinsically fun (e.g., sketch a vision board for 10 minutes, experiment on a new skill, or call a supportive friend to brainstorm). **Prompt:** Review "**Tunnel Vision → Joy Drain**" to reframe how you pursue goals.

Day 5: Notice When Force Fails

Theme: Burnout Cycles (Chapter 3)

Activity:

Rate your current energy on a scale from 1–10.

Identify one area where you've been forcing progress (e.g., working extra hours, over-scheduling, or ignoring rest).

Schedule a **10-minute strategic pause** today – take a short walk, do a guided breathing exercise, or simply sit quietly.

Prompt: Recall Alex's story of burnout and note which signs you might be overlooking in your own life.

Day 6: Observe Nature's Flexibility

Theme: Trees That Bend (Chapter 4)

Activity:

Spend 5–10 minutes outside (or look at images of willow/bamboo online). Observe how branches yield to wind.

In your journal, ask: "Where in my life can I yield rather than force?"

Prompt: Let the "Bending Tree" metaphor show how adaptive flexibility conserves energy.

Day 7: Introduce Strategic Stillness

Theme: Pause Before Reacting (Chapter 9)

Activity:

Block out 15 minutes today for **pure stillness** – no screens, no tasks, just quiet observation or breathing.

Journal: "What surfaced when I paused? What did I notice about my usual habits or thoughts?"

Prompt: Practice **"Take a Breath, Don't React"** to build self-regulation skills.

Week 2: Cultivating Resilience

Day 8: Reframe Detours

Theme: The Detour Is Not the End (Chapter 5)

Activity:

Recall a recent setback or unexpected change (big or small).

Brainstorm three alternative routes you could take instead of forcing your original plan.

Prompt: Draw on Marcus's pivot story to see how obstacles become invitations for course correction.

Day 9: Practice Emotional Agility – Observe Emotions

Theme: Naming and Befriending Feelings (Chapter 8)

Activity:

Throughout today, when a strong emotion arises, pause and silently label it ("This is frustration," "This is joy").

Breathe into that emotion for 30 seconds without judgment.

Journal briefly: "What did I learn by naming that feeling?"

Prompt: Follow the first two steps of "**Show Up → Step Out → Get Curious → Values-Based Move**".

Day 10: Emotional Agility Check-In

Theme: From Automatic Reaction to Values-Based Response (Toolkit)

Activity:

Copy or download the **Emotional Agility Check-In worksheet** (trigger → feeling → need → micro-move) from the bonus toolkit.

Fill it out based on a recent tough moment. Then, enact the micro-move you identified.

Prompt: Notice how naming your needs and choosing even a tiny action changes your trajectory.

Day 11: Affirm Your Purpose Statement

Theme: Purpose Over Plan (Chapter 7)

Activity:

Craft a one-sentence **Purpose Statement**:

"I exist to _____ because _____."

Spend 5 minutes reflecting on how that statement transcends any single goal.

Prompt: Lean on Chapter 7's guidance about anchoring to values rather than outcomes.

Day 12: Generate Creative Alternatives

Theme: Creative Rerouting (Chapter 10)

Activity:

Identify a current problem (work project, habit you want to change, or relationship tension).

Brainstorm **three completely different solutions** – even if they seem impractical.

Commit to testing one in a small way before the end of this week.

Prompt: Use the **3Rs framework (Recognize → Reimagine → Re-engage)** to structure your alternatives.

Day 13: Implement a Growth Micro-Move

Theme: Small Shifts, Big Impact (Chapter 11)

Activity:

Choose one area for improvement – health, learning, or connection.

Define a micro-move (e.g., drink one extra glass of water, read two pages of a new book send a "thinking of you" message to a friend).

Execute and track that micro-move today.

Prompt: Remember how micro-wins build momentum over time (see "Micro-Move Method").

Day 14: Map Your Personal Ecosystem

Theme: Building Your Personal Ecosystem (Chapter 13)

Activity:

List your five closest daily contacts (people you spend the most time with: friends, family, colleagues). Next to each name, note whether they generally:

☑ LIFT YOU UP (+) or

☒ DRAIN YOU (−)

Then, reflect:

☑ NURTURE the relationships that uplift you.

☑ SET A BOUNDARY or limit time with those who consistently drain your energy.

Finally, audit your **routines, environments**, and **information diet:**

☑ ROUTINES: Which daily or weekly habits ground you? Which habits exhaust you?

✅ ENVIRONMENTS: Where do you feel most alive? Where do you feel most depleted?

✅ INFORMATION DIET: What news feeds, newsletters, or social streams do you consume every day? Which inspire growth, and which create negativity?

Prompt: Use Chapter 13's guidance: – "Your personal ecosystem is everything around you that shapes mindset, motivation, and energy. Curate people, routines, environments, and inputs to sustain your flexible life"

Week 3: Deepening Adaptive Practices

Day 15: Rooted Yet Flexible

Theme: Lessons from Roots and Wind (Chapter 6)

Activity:

During a 5-minute walk (or via a brief visualization), imagine your "roots" winding around rocks and seeking nourishment in fresh soil.

Journal: "What obstacles (rocks) am I now bypassing by rerouting my roots?"

Prompt: Revisit **"Roots Seek New Paths"** and **"Water Embraces Fluidity"** to inform how you navigate blockages.

Day 16: Deepen Strategic Stillness

Theme: Regular Pauses (Chapter 9)

Activity:

Schedule two **5-minute mindfulness breaks** today – one mid-morning, one mid-afternoon. Remove all devices, sit quietly, and focus only on your breath.

After each break, jot down any insight or feeling of calm you experienced.

Prompt: Compare to Day 7's stillness: how do these shorter, repeated pauses shift your day?

Day 17: Turn Feedback into Growth

Theme: Reframing Setbacks (Chapter 10)

Activity:

Choose a recent perceived failure or criticism.

List **three lessons** it offered you.

Write one **next action** that integrates those lessons – even if it's just a single-sentence plan.

Prompt: Use the **"Reframe Failure"** mindset to convert disappointment into actionable data.

Day 18: Purpose-Centred Choices

Theme: Aligning Actions with Your Purpose (Chapter 7)

Activity:

Throughout today, before making any significant choice, pause and ask:

"Does this align with my Purpose Statement?"

Note any moments you felt a tug in the opposite direction and how you responded (e.g., "I said no because it clashed with my values").

Prompt: Recall that intentionally anchoring in purpose helps you bend without breaking.

Day 19: Emotional Agility in Conversation

Theme: Surfing Emotions with Others (Chapter 8)

Activity:

In a dialogue where emotions run high (a work discussion or family conversation), practice:

✅ NAME-IT: "I notice I feel irritated."

✅ STEP-OUT: Take a breath.

✅ GET CURIOUS: Ask yourself: "Why is this emotion here?"

✅ VALUES-BASED MOVE: Respond in line with what truly matters (e.g., speak calmly, ask a clarifying question).

Journal: "How did naming and curiosity shift the tone of that conversation?"

Prompt: Lean on the Emotional Agility toolkit for real-time practice.

Day 20: Pilot an Innovation Plan

Theme: Creative Rerouting in Action (Chapter 10)

Activity:

Choose a real-world area where you feel stuck (job, creative project, habit).

Create a **mini "Innovation Plan":**

✅ DEFINE THE BLOCK in one sentence.

✅ BRAINSTORM three unconventional approaches.

✅ PICK ONE to prototype or test this weekend.

Prompt: Draw inspiration from Jake's and Sarah's small-shift stories to see how tiny creative tweaks can redirect momentum.

Day 21: Integration Rituals Kick-off

Theme: Rituals for Ongoing Growth (Chapter 14)

Activity:

Review the **Integration Rituals table** (examples: Sunday Reset, Morning Centring, Weekly Review, etc.).

Choose **one ritual** you can realistically sustain (e.g., a daily two-minute morning pause, a weekly Friday reflection). Schedule it in your calendar.

Prompt: Integration isn't overwhelm - start with exactly one practice you know you'll maintain.

Week 4: Living the Breeze

Day 22: Savor the Process

Theme: Presence Over Perpetual Future (Chapter 10)

Activity:

Choose one mundane routine today (eating breakfast, washing dishes, commuting). Slow it down - focus on each sensory detail (sight, sound, texture, taste, smell).

Journal: "What did I notice when I wasn't rushing? How did it feel?"

Prompt: Recall Evan's story of learning to enjoy the present instead of chasing the next milestone.

Day 23: Double Down on Micro-Moves

Theme: Scaling Through Consistency (Chapter 11)

Activity:

Revisit the micro-move you implemented on Day 13. **Double it** today (e.g., if you read two pages, read four; if you sent one message, send two).

Observe how a slightly larger commitment still feels manageable.

Prompt: Reflect on Omar's Tiny Habit: a 15-minute nightly sketch became a business over time.

Day 24: Curate Your Attention

Theme: Protect Your Mental Ecosystem (Chapter 12)

Activity:

Audit your digital inputs: unsubscribe from or mute one draining newsletter or social feed.

Replace 10 minutes of "doom-scrolling" with 10 minutes of an inspiring podcast, article, or book excerpt.

Prompt: Remember Layla's story – small changes in "inputs" led to major life shifts.

Day 25: Revisit and Refine Your Purpose

Theme: Evolving North Star (Chapter 7)

Activity:

Re-read your Purpose Statement from Day 11. Edit any words to reflect how you've learned or shifted during these past weeks.

Journal: "How has my sense of purpose deepened or changed?"

Prompt: Purpose evolves – honour how your values have clarified over the first 24 days.

Day 26: Iterate on Innovation Experiments

Theme: Feedback Loops and Adaptation (Chapter 10)

Activity:

Review the three creative alternatives you brainstormed on Day 20. For each, note:

☑ WHAT WORKED?

☑ WHAT SURPRISE EMERGED?

☑ WHAT TWEAK WILL YOU TEST NEXT?

Plan how you'll implement that tweak within the next week.

Prompt: Leverage feedback loops (trial → reflection → adjust) to keep refining solutions.

Day 27: Deep Strategic Stillness

Theme: Active Pausing (Chapter 9)

Activity:

Block a **30-minute "Silent Retreat"** – no phone, no tasks, just sitting or gentle walking.

Afterward, journal: "What internal guidance emerged when I removed distractions?"

Prompt: Embrace stillness as a proactive strategy, not avoidance.

Day 28: Build Accountability Partnerships

Theme: Community Support (Chapter 12)

Activity:

Invite a friend or colleague to discuss one insight from this challenge. Share where you're stretching and ask for their perspective.

Commit to a **bi-weekly check-in** on shared goals or micro-moves.

Prompt: Rely on accountability relationships to maintain your "breeze" mindset.

Final Two Days: Consolidate and Celebrate

Day 29: Reflect and Commit Forward

Theme: Anchoring Key Practices (Conclusion & Chapter 15)

Activity:

Re-read the final blessing: "Be the flower that bends."

Write a **"Letter to Future You"** highlighting **three core practices** you commit to sustaining (e.g., "I will pause daily," "I will schedule weekly ecosystem audits," "I will craft a micro-move each Monday").

Prompt: Use Chapter 15's flower-and-storm metaphor to inspire enduring resilience.

Day 30: Celebrate Milestones and Plan Next Steps

Theme: Transition from Challenge to Lifestyle

Activity:

Review all your daily journals, worksheets, or notes. Highlight key breakthroughs, shifts in mindset, and practices that felt most impactful.

Design a **30-Day "Graduation" Ritual** (e.g., lighting a candle, sharing your journey with a friend, or treating yourself to something meaningful).

Outline **Next 30 Days of Micro-Moves** that will sustain this momentum (e.g., a weekly stillness session, daily 1-minute mindfulness, monthly ecosystem check-ins).

Prompt: Celebrate your resilience. Acknowledge how far you've come – and commit to continuing the breeze mindset.